The Yeti, Russian Yeti, Sasquatch & Bigfoot - A Mystery in many Guises

Echoes in the Snow

Gordon Kean Clarke

S.D.N Publishing

Copyright © 2024 – SDN Publishing

All rights reserved.

No portion of this book may be reproduced in any form without written permission from the publisher or author, except as permitted by U.S. copyright law.

ISBN: 9798883690678

General Disclaimer

This book is intended to provide informative and educational material on the subject matter covered. The author(s), publisher, and any affiliated parties make no representations or warranties with respect to the accuracy, applicability, completeness, or suitability of the contents herein and specifically disclaim any implied warranties of merchantability or fitness for a particular purpose.

The information contained in this book is for general information purposes only and is not intended to serve as legal, medical, financial, or any other form of professional advice. Readers should consult with appropriate professionals before making any decisions based on the information provided. Neither the author(s) nor the publisher shall be held responsible or liable for any loss, damage, injury, claim, or otherwise, whether direct or indirect, consequential, or incidental, that may occur as a result of applying or misinterpreting the information in this book.

This book may contain references to third-party websites, products, or services. Such references do not constitute an endorsement or recommendation, and the author(s) and publisher are not responsible for any outcomes related to these third-party references.

In no event shall the author(s), publisher, or any affiliated parties be liable for any direct, indirect, punitive, special, incidental, or other consequential damages arising directly or indirectly from any use of this material, which is provided "as is," and without warranties of any kind, express or implied.

By reading this book, you acknowledge and agree that you assume all risks and responsibilities concerning the applicability and consequences of the information provided. You also agree to

THE YETI, RUSSIAN YETI, SASQUATCH & BIGFOOT...

indemnify, defend, and hold harmless the author(s), publisher, and any affiliated parties from any and all liabilities, claims, demands, actions, and causes of action whatsoever, whether or not foreseeable, that may arise from using or misusing the information contained in this book.

Although every effort has been made to ensure the accuracy of the information in this book as of the date of publication, the landscape of the subject matter covered is continuously evolving. Therefore, the author(s) and publisher expressly disclaim responsibility for any errors or omissions and reserve the right to update, alter, or revise the content without prior notice.

By continuing to read this book, you agree to be bound by the terms and conditions stated in this disclaimer. If you do not agree with these terms, it is your responsibility to discontinue use of this book immediately.

Contents

1. Foreword from the Author ... 1
2. The Yeti - A Mystery in many Guises ... 3
3. Ecology, Environment and Early Encounters with the Yeti ... 22
4. Yeti Encounter 1 - The Andes Expedition ... 39
5. Analyzing the Yeti Evidence ... 46
6. Psychological, Sociological and Economic Impact of the Yeti ... 70
7. Yeti Encounter 2 - The Slopes of Everest ... 85
8. The Yeti in Global Media - A Study of Representation ... 93
9. Philosophical Perspectives: Myth and Reality ... 114
10. Yeti Encounter 3 - The Russian Enigma ... 135
11. Debunking Yeti Myths: A Scientific Approach ... 145
12. The Ecological Impact of Cryptids ... 165
13. Modern Mythology ... 173
14. Concluding Echoes: The Lasting Mystery of the Yeti ... 191

Chapter 1
Foreword from the Author

Welcome to a journey through the enigmatic and captivating world of the Yeti, a creature that has long captured human imagination and curiosity. This book aims to provide an extensive exploration of the various facets of the Yeti phenomenon, encompassing a wide range of subject areas and delving deep into the cultural, historical, and scientific narratives that surround this mythical creature.

Our exploration is not just confined to collating detailed and established information about the Yeti. One of the unique aspects of this book is the inclusion of three previously unpublished encounters with the Yeti. These accounts, which have been shared with us under the condition of anonymity, offer intriguing and personal experiences of individuals who claim to have come face-to-face with this legendary being. To protect the privacy and safety of these individuals, we have altered names and certain specific locations in their stories. While the authenticity of these encounters cannot be independently verified, and the author cannot confirm the veracity of the claims made, they nevertheless provide fascinating insights into the enduring allure and mystery of the Yeti.

This book is structured to provide a comprehensive understanding of the Yeti, integrating perspectives from folklore, anthropology, history, and cryptozoology. The aim is to not only present the diverse cultural and historical contexts in which the Yeti is situated but also to explore the scientific investigations and debates that have attempted to unravel its existence. From the Himalayas, where the Yeti is deeply rooted in the traditions and spiritual beliefs of local communities, to its portrayal in Western media and popular culture, this book seeks to cover all dimensions of the Yeti's place in human culture.

The Yeti, often regarded as a bridge between the known and the unknown, serves as a powerful symbol of the mysteries that still lie unexplored in our world. Whether viewed through the lens of skepticism or belief, the stories and research presented in this book aim to enrich our understanding of this enigmatic creature and its impact on human thought and imagination.

As you turn the pages, we invite you to keep an open mind and embark on this fascinating exploration of one of the most intriguing mysteries of our time – the Yeti. Let the journey begin.

Chapter 2
The Yeti - A Mystery in many Guises

The legend of the Yeti, also known as the Abominable Snowman, has been a captivating mystery, especially in the context of Russian and Himalayan folklore. The Yeti, an ape-like creature purported to inhabit the Himalayan mountain range, has long been a subject of intrigue and speculation, particularly in the Western world.

Historically, the Yeti was perceived quite differently in various cultures. In Bhutanese folklore, Yetis were believed to perform nocturnal caretaking duties at a temple devoted to Panden Lhamo, a protection deity, signifying their benevolent nature. This depiction contrasts sharply with the Western image of the Yeti as a monstrous being. The Western perception originated from a misinterpretation of the term "metoh-kangmi" by journalist Henry Newman in 1921, who translated it as "abominable snowman," thereby casting the Yeti in a much more menacing light.

In Tibetan lore, the Yeti is known by different names and characteristics. The Lepcha people of eastern Nepal, western Bhutan, and West Bengal in India, refer to the Yeti as Chu Mung or "Glacier Spirit," a god of the hunt and the creatures of the forest. They believe that Chu Mung can resurrect incomplete animal carcasses, a belief that influences their hunting rituals and perceptions of the natural world.

Folklorists trace the origins of the Yeti to a mix of factors, including Sherpa folklore and potentially misidentified fauna like bears or yaks. The Yeti is often described as a large, bipedal ape-like creature covered in hair, and it's compared to similar cryptids like North America's Bigfoot.

Recent scientific investigations have provided a more rational explanation for the Yeti legends. An international team of scientists conducted DNA analysis on artifacts purported to be body parts of the Yeti. Their findings, published in a scientific journal, revealed that these artifacts actually belonged to various species of bears native to the Himalayan region. This research not only debunked many myths surrounding the Yeti but also contributed to the understanding of the lineage of brown bears in the region.

The legend of the Yeti, spanning thousands of years, has played a significant role in the folklore and culture of the Himalayan regions. Despite scientific debunking, the Yeti remains an important cultural symbol and a subject of fascination in both Eastern and Western societies. Its mythological stature endures, illustrating the human propensity for mystery and the unknown.

Understanding the Yeti phenomenon through these varied lenses—folkloric, historical, and scientific—provides a comprehensive picture of how this legendary creature has been perceived and interpreted across different cultures and times. This mythical creature, once believed to roam the snowy landscapes of the Himalayas and even the remote regions of Russia, serves as a fascinating example of how folklore can intersect with science and culture, shaping our understanding of the natural world and the mysteries it holds.

Legends of the Taiga: Ancient Folklore

In the realm of ancient folklore, the Yeti holds a prominent place, especially within Tibetan traditions. These legends paint a vastly different picture compared to the Western view of the Yeti as a monstrous creature. In Tibet, Yetis were seen as benevolent beings, sometimes even participating in Buddhist rituals. For instance, a 17th-century Sherpa religious leader recounted how a Yeti cared for him while he meditated in a cave, bringing him sustenance and learning Buddhist ways, ultimately becoming a disciple. This Yeti, upon its death, was honored with its remains placed in a monastery as sacred relics.

Furthermore, in Bhutan, folklore suggests that Yetis would undertake nocturnal temple caretaking duties, highlighting their revered status within the community. These stories often depict Yetis as kind, intelligent beings, a contrast to their portrayal in Western narratives. Yetis in Himalayan countries were known for their kindness, helping lost travelers in the mountains, a trait that elevated them above mere animals in cultural perceptions.

The transformation of the Yeti's image in the West can be traced back to a mistranslation by journalist Henry Newman in 1921, who coined the term "abominable snowman," thereby altering its perception from a benevolent being to a fearsome monster. This shift in perception underscores the impact of cultural interpretations on folklore.

In other regions, like among the Lepcha people, the Yeti, known as Chu Mung or "Glacier Spirit," is revered as a god of the hunt and forest creatures. Their folklore includes rituals and beliefs centered around the Yeti, further illustrating the creature's integration into their cultural and spiritual life.

These diverse and rich folklore traditions offer a fascinating glimpse into how the Yeti has been perceived across different cultures, ranging from a revered spiritual entity to a mysterious cryptid in Western narratives.

Cultural Echoes: Yeti in Siberian Culture

The cultural impact of the Yeti in Siberian folklore and society is a complex and multi-layered phenomenon. This narrative begins deep within the historical context of Siberia, where the Yeti, known locally as "Chuchunaa" or "Snow Man," has long been part of the folklore. These stories depict the Yeti as a creature of the wilderness, embodying the mysterious and untamed spirit of Siberia's vast landscapes.

Local accounts often describe the Yeti as a large, human-like being covered in fur, with immense physical strength and an elusive nature. These descriptions vary, with some portraying the Yeti as a benign entity, while others cast it in a more ominous light. The Yeti's presence in these tales often serves as a reminder of the unexplored and wild aspects of Siberia, where nature remains dominant and humans are mere visitors.

In more recent times, alleged sightings and encounters have added a layer of intrigue to the Yeti's story in Siberia. These incidents, often reported in remote areas, have not only sustained the folklore but also attracted attention from the global community, including researchers and enthusiasts of cryptozoology. Each reported sighting brings a surge of interest, sparking debates and discussions about the existence of such a creature.

The Yeti's cultural significance in Siberia extends beyond mere folklore. It symbolizes the relationship between humans and the natural world, serving as a metaphor for the unknown and the mysteries that the vast Siberian wilderness holds. The Yeti represents the untamed and unexplored, challenging the boundaries of our understanding and inviting us to consider the possibilities that lie beyond the known world.

In modern Siberian society, the Yeti also plays a role in regional tourism. The intrigue surrounding this legendary creature draws visitors eager to explore the remote areas where sightings have been reported. This interest has a tangible impact on local communities, contributing to the economy and fostering a unique cultural exchange centered around the myth of the Yeti.

To understand the Yeti's place in Siberian culture, it is essential to look at both the historical folklore and the contemporary narratives that continue to shape its legend. The Yeti is more than a mythical creature; it is a symbol of the wild, uncharted territories that still exist in our world and the enduring human fascination with the mysteries of nature.

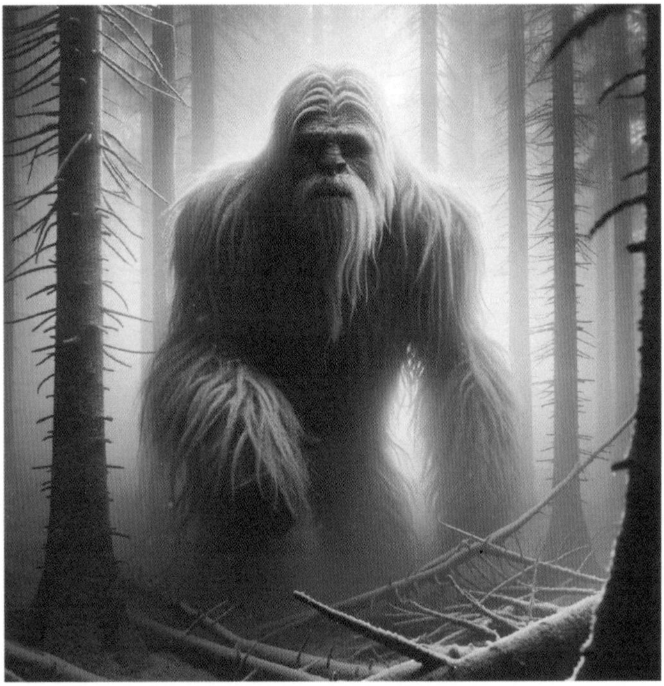

The Yeti in Folklore and Oral Traditions: A Global View

The Yeti, a creature steeped in mystery and allure, holds a significant place in the folklore and oral traditions across the globe. This enigmatic being, known in the Himalayas as the formidable "Abominable Snowman," presents a fascinating contrast in its portrayal across different cultures. While in some Eastern cultures, the Yeti is seen as a benign entity, symbolizing the spirit of nature and wilderness, in others, it is depicted as a fearsome and elusive creature. These divergent narratives offer a rich tapestry of stories and beliefs, reflecting each culture's unique relationship with their environment and the unknown.

1. The Yeti in Himalayan Folklore

In the rugged terrains of the Himalayas, the Yeti is often depicted as the "Abominable Snowman," a formidable being inhabiting the remote, snow-covered mountains. This portrayal likely stems from the region's harsh environmental conditions, where the Yeti is envisaged as a powerful and sometimes threatening presence. The Himalayan narratives often imbue the Yeti with characteristics that command respect and caution, serving as a reminder of the unpredictable forces of nature.

2. Eastern Perspectives on the Yeti

Contrasting with the Himalayan view, other Eastern cultures depict the Yeti in a more benevolent light. Here, it is often seen as a guardian of the mountains or a gentle giant, symbolizing the deep connection between humans and the natural world. These interpretations reflect a more harmonious view of the Yeti, one that emphasizes coexistence and respect for the wilderness. This portrayal resonates with the spiritual and animistic beliefs prevalent in many Eastern cultures, where every element of nature is believed to have a spirit or deity associated with it.

3. The Yeti in Western Narratives

In Western interpretations, influenced by early explorers' tales and media portrayals, the Yeti often assumes a more ominous and threatening persona. Here, it is a creature of mystery and danger, an embodiment of the wild unknown that beckons the brave and adventurous. This depiction reflects a more confrontational relationship with the unknown, where the Yeti symbolizes a challenge to be overcome or a mystery to be solved.

4. Modern Evolution of the Yeti's Image

In contemporary times, the Yeti transcends its mythological roots to become a subject of scientific and pop culture fascination. The quest to prove or debunk its existence has sparked numerous scientific expeditions and studies, utilizing technologies like DNA analysis. This scientific interest showcases our inherent curiosity and the power of folklore to inspire rigorous inquiry. Moreover, the Yeti's portrayal in media and literature has diversified its image, transforming it from a mythical creature into a symbol of nature's mysteries and wonders. Its presence in films, books, and other media often embodies themes of exploration and mankind's confrontation with nature.

These varying portrayals of the Yeti, from a symbol of spiritual reverence in Eastern cultures to a figure of adventure and scientific curiosity in the West, highlight the diverse ways societies interpret and interact with the mysteries of their world. The Yeti, in its many forms, continues to captivate our imagination, serving as a reminder of the enduring allure of the unknown and the profound impact of folklore on our understanding of the world around us.

Comparative Mythology: Yeti Across Cultures

In exploring the comparative mythology of the Yeti across various cultures, we uncover a rich tapestry of beliefs and narratives. This cryptid, known by different names like Bigfoot in North America and the Yowie in Australia, often represents a deep connection with the untamed natural world. These stories, deeply rooted in indigenous cultures, serve various functions ranging from explaining natural phenomena to imparting moral lessons.

In North American folklore, Bigfoot is often depicted as a reclusive giant inhabiting remote forests, symbolizing humanity's lost connection with nature. The Native American interpretations vary widely, with some tribes viewing Bigfoot as a spiritual entity, while others regard it as a physical creature.

The Australian Yowie, similar to the Yeti and Bigfoot, is ingrained in Aboriginal folklore. Descriptions of the Yowie vary, but it's often portrayed as a hairy, ape-like creature living in the wilderness, embodying the mysteries of the Australian outback.

These diverse cultural narratives highlight the universal human fascination with the unknown and the wilderness. The Yeti, Bigfoot, and Yowie are not just mythical creatures; they represent the unexplored, the mysterious aspects of our world that remain just beyond our understanding. They invite us to look closer at our surroundings and question what might be lurking in the uncharted corners of our planet.

Thus, the comparative study of the Yeti across cultures provides insights into humanity's relationship with the natural world and its mysteries. It reveals how different societies use folklore to make sense of the unknown and express their intrinsic connection to the environment.

The Yeti in Comparative Mythology: Global Perspectives

The Yeti, a creature steeped in mystery, has captured the imagination of various cultures around the world, each adding its unique interpretation to the legend. Let's delve into the Yeti's portrayal in global mythology, revealing a fascinating array of narratives that reflect diverse cultural attitudes toward this enigmatic being.

In Tibetan folklore, the Yeti, often referred to as the "Abominable Snowman," is deeply ingrained in the region's cultural and spiritual fabric. Derived from the Tibetan words "yeh-teh" or "na-lmo," meaning "rock bear," the Yeti is perceived as a powerful, ape-like creature residing in the high-altitude mountain regions. Tibetan culture often depicts the Yeti as a guardian spirit of the Himalayan peaks, symbolizing the untamed and wild nature of the high-altitude wilderness. The

Yeti is not just a cryptid in Tibetan folklore; it holds a significant place in the cultural and spiritual traditions of the region, sometimes even associated with Tibetan Buddhism practices.

The Western perception of the Yeti, particularly in the early 20th century, was largely shaped by explorers' accounts and sensationalized media portrayals. The term "Abominable Snowman" first appeared in 1921 when Charles Howard-Bury led the British Mount Everest Reconnaissance Expedition and recorded an account of large footprints in his book, "Mount Everest – The Reconnaissance." These footprints were attributed by the Sherpa guides to "The Wild Man of the Snows," which they called "metoh-kangmi" ("Metoh" meaning "man-bear" and "Kang-mi" meaning "snowman"). This Western depiction often presents the Yeti as a white, ape-like creature, which contrasts with the original descriptions of the Yeti being covered in brown, reddish, or black fur.

The pursuit of the Yeti has led to various sightings and explorations in the 20th century. One notable incident was Sir Edmund Hillary and Tenzing Norgay's claim of encountering large footprints while scaling Mount Everest in 1953, which significantly contributed to the creature's mystique. Other instances include the sighting by photographer N.A. Tombazi near the Zemu Glacier and the famous footprints photographed by Eric Shipton in 1951. Despite these accounts, most scientific investigations have not provided concrete evidence of the Yeti's existence, often attributing findings to known animals like bears.

In popular culture, the Yeti has transcended its origins in folklore, appearing in films, books, and television shows, symbolizing the allure of the unexplored and the unknown. Its image as a towering, ape-like creature with shaggy fur has become emblematic of humanity's enduring fascination with the mysteries of nature.

The Yeti's portrayal in comparative mythology illustrates the diverse ways in which different cultures perceive and interact with the mysteries of their world. From a guardian spirit in Tibetan culture to a sensationalized cryptid in Western narratives, the Yeti continues to captivate and intrigue, embodying humanity's quest to understand the unknown.

Anthropological Insights: The Yeti's Place

The anthropological study of the Yeti phenomenon provides a unique lens through which to view human cultural and social dynamics. This mysterious creature, rooted in folklore yet engaging the interest of modern science, serves as a powerful symbol across various societies.

The Yeti in Traditional Societies In traditional Himalayan societies, the Yeti is more than a mere legend. It is often intertwined with spiritual beliefs and local customs. The Sherpas and other indigenous groups of the Himalayas, for instance, regard the Yeti as an integral part of their natural and spiritual landscape. It is seen not just as a physical entity but as a guardian of the mountains, a being that commands respect and awe. This reverence for the Yeti reflects a broader respect for the environment, a recognition of the power and mystery of nature.

Yeti: A Cultural Conduit In Western societies, the Yeti often embodies the allure of the unknown and the thrill of exploration. Early Western expeditions in search of the Yeti were not just scientific endeavors; they were cultural encounters that reflected the West's fascination with 'exotic' lands and their mysteries. The Yeti thus serves as a conduit through which different cultures express and negotiate their understanding of the 'other'.

Scientific Investigations and Debates Anthropologists and other scientists have taken an interest in the Yeti as part of a broader exploration of human belief systems and myth-making practices. The scientific study of the Yeti - involving field expeditions, analysis of alleged Yeti evidence, and discussions in cryptozoology - also sheds light on how scientific communities interact with folklore and legend. These investigations, while often skeptical and evidence-driven, underscore the enduring human fascination with myths and the unexplained.

The Yeti in Global Media and Public Imagination The Yeti's portrayal in global media - from sensationalist reports to appearances in movies and literature - reflects and shapes public perceptions of this creature. This portrayal often says more about the society creating these media than about the Yeti itself. In popular culture, the Yeti is a canvas onto which various fears, curiosities, and fantasies are projected.

The Yeti's place in anthropology reveals the complex ways in which human societies construct and interact with myths. It highlights the intersections between culture, belief, and the natural world. Whether regarded as a sacred guardian, a mysterious cryptid, or a cultural icon, the Yeti remains a compelling subject in the study of human societies and their mythologies.

Anthropological Studies of Yeti Legends: Cultural Significance

The legend of the Yeti, woven into the fabric of various cultures, offers a unique anthropological study. This elusive creature, known in different regions under various names such as Bigfoot or Sasquatch in North America and Yowie in Australia, is not merely a cryptid but a cultural symbol, deeply embedded in the folklore and collective psyche of the societies that narrate its existence.

The Yeti in Tibetan Culture In Tibetan culture, the Yeti, also known as the "Abominable Snowman," is deeply embedded in both folklore and mythology. The Yeti in Tibetan lore is more than a cryptid; it holds a significant place in cultural and spiritual traditions. Considered a guardian spirit of the Himalayan peaks, the Yeti symbolizes the untamed and wild nature of high-altitude wilderness. It embodies the idea that there are still mysteries and unexplored realms within the natural world. Tibetan folklore also views encounters with the Yeti as a test of courage and resilience, with those who survive such encounters believed to be blessed with strength and wisdom. The Yeti is thought to possess supernatural abilities and is sometimes associated with Tibetan Buddhism practices.

Western Perceptions and Encounters The Western perception of the Yeti, shaped by early explorers' tales and media portrayals, presents it as a fearsome and elusive creature. The term "Abominable Snowman" was first used in the early 20th century by Western explorers venturing into the Himalayas, leading to tales of encounters with a giant, shaggy, human-like creature. These narratives reflect the West's fascination with 'exotic' lands and their mysteries, casting the Yeti as a symbol of the wild unknown, a challenge to be faced by the daring. The Yeti, in these narratives, becomes a bridge through which different cultures express and negotiate their understanding of the 'other'.

Anthropological Perspectives From an anthropological viewpoint, the Yeti serves as a compelling subject in understanding how societies construct and interact with myths. It highlights the intersections between culture, belief, and the natural world. The Yeti's portrayal in different cultures offers insights into humanity's relationship with nature and the unknown. Whether regarded as a sacred guardian, a mysterious cryptid, or a cultural icon, the Yeti remains a powerful symbol in the study of human societies and their mythologies.

The anthropological study of Yeti legends underscores the complex and multifaceted nature of human beliefs and cultural narratives. It reveals how myths and folklore can provide a deeper understanding of societal values, fears, and aspirations. The Yeti, in its various cultural incarnations, serves as a mirror reflecting the diverse ways in which humans perceive and interact with the mysteries of their world.

Myth in Depth: Anthropological Perspectives

The anthropological exploration of the Yeti legend delves into how this mythical creature is deeply rooted in various cultures, serving as a powerful symbol that resonates with human experiences and beliefs.

The Yeti in Tibetan Mythology In Tibetan mythology, the Yeti, also known as the "Abominable Snowman," occupies a significant place. The term "Yeti" is derived from Tibetan words translating to "rock bear," reflecting its perceived nature as a powerful, ape-like creature in high-altitude mountains. In Tibetan folklore, the Yeti is not merely a cryptid but a guardian spirit of the Himalayan peaks, a symbol of the untamed and wild nature of these wilderness areas. The Yeti is associated with tests of courage and resilience, with those encountering it believed to gain strength and wisdom. Some Tibetans also see the Yeti as a link between physical and spiritual realms, possessing supernatural abilities and sometimes associated with Tibetan Buddhism.

Western Interpretation of the Yeti The Western perception of the Yeti differs significantly. The term "Abominable Snowman" emerged in the early 20th century, colored by Western explorers' accounts and sensationalized media portrayals. This depiction often paints the Yeti as a white, ape-like creature, contrasting with original descriptions of it being covered in brown, reddish, or black fur. The Western narrative often positions the Yeti as a symbol of the unexplored and the unknown, reflecting a fascination with 'exotic' lands and their mysteries.

Anthropological Relevance Anthropologically, the Yeti serves as a fascinating subject for understanding human belief systems and myth-making practices. It highlights how scientific communities interact with folklore and legend, underscoring human curiosity about myths and the unexplained. The Yeti's portrayal in global media, including films, books, and television shows, reflects and shapes public perceptions, revealing more about the society creating these narratives than about the Yeti itself.

The anthropological study of the Yeti legend underscores the complex interplay between culture, belief, and the natural world. It reveals how myths and folklore provide a deeper understanding of societal values, fears, and aspirations. Whether as a sacred guardian, a mysterious cryptid, or a cultural icon, the Yeti remains a compelling symbol in the study of human societies and their relationship with the mysteries of their world.

The Yeti in Ethnographic Studies: Indigenous Beliefs and Practices

The ethnographic details surrounding the Yeti in Himalayan societies offer a rich tapestry of cultural beliefs, practices, and narratives. These details not only provide a deeper understanding of the Yeti's place in the Himalayas but also reflect the complex relationship between these communities and their environment.

Rituals and Spiritual Beliefs

In Himalayan communities, particularly those practicing the pre-Buddhist Bön religion, the Yeti is deeply woven into spiritual beliefs. Rituals often involved honoring the Yeti, seen as a guardian or deity-like figure. For example, annual sacrifices were made to appease the Yeti for protection and good fortune. In certain ceremonies, offerings such as food or symbolic objects were laid out in specific patterns as a gesture of reverence or to seek blessings from the Yeti, believed to be a powerful spirit of the mountains.

Folklore and Storytelling

The Yeti occupies a prominent place in local folklore, often portrayed as a powerful and mysterious creature living in remote mountainous regions. Storytelling, an integral part of Himalayan culture, features the Yeti in various narratives, from cautionary tales to accounts of encounters. Elders in the community often recount these tales to younger generations, not just as entertainment but as a means of imparting moral lessons and cultural values. These stories serve to instill respect for the natural world and its unseen forces, with the Yeti often symbolizing the wild and untamed aspects of nature.

Symbolism and Cultural Identity

For many Himalayan communities, the Yeti is more than a mythical creature; it symbolizes their cultural identity and their deep connection to the land. The Yeti represents the mysteries and wonders of the Himalayas, embodying the spirit of these rugged and majestic landscapes. In local art and cultural expressions, representations of the Yeti are common, showcasing the creature's significance in the collective psyche of these communities.

Community Encounters and Perceptions

Accounts of Yeti encounters, though varied, form an essential part of local lore. Some describe the Yeti as a shy and elusive creature, while others portray it as a more ominous presence. These accounts, often passed down through generations, are not merely tales but part of the lived experience and oral history of the communities. The Yeti is perceived differently across various villages and regions, reflecting the diverse ecological and cultural landscapes of the Himalayas.

Impact on Local Practices

The Yeti also influences certain local practices, such as hunting and nature conservation. In some communities, areas believed to be inhabited by the Yeti are often left undisturbed, stemming from a mix of reverence and fear. This has inadvertently led to the conservation of certain remote and pristine areas of the forest and mountain ecosystems.

By examining these ethnographic details, we gain a richer understanding of how the Yeti is deeply embedded in the cultural fabric of Himalayan societies. This mythical creature is not just a subject of fascination but a significant element that shapes the cultural, spiritual, and environmental consciousness of these communities.

Chapter 3
Ecology, Environment and Early Encounters with the Yeti

The Ecology of Siberia: An Overview

The ecology of Siberia, a vast region extending from the Ural Mountains in the west to the Pacific Ocean in the east and from the Arctic Ocean to the borders of Kazakhstan, Mongolia, and China, is both complex and diverse. It encompasses a total area of about 5.2 million square miles, with the Russian portion alone covering around 2.5 million square miles. Siberia is divided into four major geographic regions: the West Siberian Plain, Central Siberia, Northeastern Siberia, and the Baikal area. Each region boasts distinct ecological features.

In the west, adjacent to the Ural Mountains, lies the expansive West Siberian Plain, characterized by its flat terrain and extensive swamplands, and drained by the Ob and Yenisey rivers. Moving eastward, Central Siberia is marked by a combination of plains and the Central Siberian Plateau. The basin of the Lena River separates Central Siberia from the intricate series of mountain ranges and basins that constitute Northeastern Siberia. The smallest of the four, the Baikal area, is centered around Lake Baikal in South-Central Siberia.

Siberia's climatic conditions are notoriously severe, with snowless yet extremely cold winters. For example, in the Sakha Republic, temperatures as low as -90°F (-68°C) have been recorded. The vegetation zones across Siberia follow an east-west extension, with tundra in the north, swampy forest or taiga across most of the region, and forest-steppe and steppe in the southwestern parts and the southern intermontane basins.

The region's rich mineral resources include coal, petroleum, natural gas, diamonds, iron ore, and gold. The latter half of the 20th century saw rapid development in both mining and manufacturing sectors, with steel, aluminum, and machinery being principal products. Agricultural activities, however, are limited to the more southern areas of Siberia, producing crops like wheat, rye, oats, and sunflowers.

Ecological Adaptations: Theoretical Perspectives

Ecological adaptations, a fundamental aspect of ecological studies, involve the intricate interplay between organisms and their environments. Theoretical perspectives in ecology provide a framework for understanding these complex relationships and adaptations.

One of the key theoretical models in understanding ecological adaptations is Bronfenbrenner's Ecological Systems Theory (EST). Originally developed to study human development, EST can be applied to ecological studies to understand how various environmental factors influence the adaptations of organisms. EST posits that there are four interconnected systems that affect development: the microsystem, mesosystem, exosystem, and macrosystem. Each system represents different levels of interaction between an organism and its environment, ranging from immediate surroundings to broader societal and cultural influences.

The microsystem encompasses the immediate environment where direct interactions occur. In an ecological context, this might include the immediate habitat and local environmental conditions that directly influence an organism's behavior and survival strategies. The mesosystem involves interactions between different microsystems, highlighting the interconnectedness of different environmental factors. For example, the relationship between a forest ecosystem and a neighboring river system can have significant implications for the species residing in both environments.

The exosystem includes broader societal factors that indirectly influence an organism, such as climate patterns or human activities that alter landscapes. These factors, while not directly interacting with the organism, can have cascading effects on its habitat and, consequently, its adaptations. Finally, the macrosystem encompasses the overarching cultural, social, and economic contexts that shape the broader environmental framework within which organisms exist.

In addition to EST, cultural adaptation theories provide insights into ecological adaptations. Cultural adaptation models, like the Markov process, examine how cultural traits evolve and adapt in response to environmental changes. This theory can be extended to ecological adaptations, where the focus is on how certain traits within a population become more prevalent due to their advantageous nature in a given environment. The probability of these adaptive traits becoming dominant in a population can be influenced by various factors, including the starting frequency of the trait and the nature of environmental changes.

Understanding ecological adaptations through these theoretical lenses allows us to appreciate the dynamic and multi-layered nature of how organisms interact with their environments. It highlights the importance of considering a wide range of factors, from immediate physical conditions to broader societal influences, in shaping the evolutionary paths of species. The interplay of these factors underscores the complexity of ecological systems and the myriad ways in which organisms adapt to survive and thrive.

Through this exploration of theoretical perspectives, we gain a deeper understanding of the nuanced and interconnected nature of ecological systems. This knowledge is crucial for informing conservation efforts, predicting responses to environmental changes, and understanding the evolutionary trajectories of various species. As we continue to face global environmental challenges, such as climate change and habitat destruction, applying these theoretical frameworks becomes increasingly important in guiding our efforts to preserve and understand the natural world.

Advanced Ecological Studies: Siberia's Environment

Advanced ecological studies of Siberia reveal a region undergoing significant environmental changes, primarily driven by climate change. Siberia, known for its vast freshwater resources, mineral wealth, and biodiversity, is experiencing rapid ecological transformations.

One of the most pressing issues in Siberia is the rate of climate change, which is occurring faster than in most other regions of the Earth. The north of Siberia is facing exceptional warming, while the south is becoming increasingly arid. This dichotomy presents unique challenges for the region's ecology and biodiversity. The warming in the north has led to an increase in forest fires, a phenomenon that is likely linked to climate change.

The political landscape in Russia, including Siberia, adds complexity to the environmental situation. There have been instances of crackdowns on Indigenous rights organizations, diminishing the capacity of Indigenous leaders to advocate for their communities and cultures in the face of climatic threats. These actions raise concerns about the preservation of Indigenous cultures, which are intimately connected with the Siberian environment.

In response to these environmental challenges, there have been shifts in governmental positions and strategies. The Russian government has begun to acknowledge the impacts of climate change, including the forest fires in Siberia. There is a push towards developing solar power stations and green hydrogen technology. However, the overall effectiveness and commitment of the Russian government to address these environmental issues remain questionable. The Climate Action Tracker, an independent climate science publication, has rated Russia's current strategy as "critically insufficient," indicating a significant gap in efforts to mitigate climate change impacts.

The energy production in Russia is also a concern. Only about 0.2 percent of Russian energy production comes from wind and solar power. While there are plans to increase the use of nuclear and hydropower, these efforts fall short of the global requirement for restraining temperature increase to 1.5 degrees Celsius, which necessitates a much higher reliance on renewables.

The situation in Siberia exemplifies the complexities of ecological change in the face of climate change, political dynamics, and socio-economic factors. These changes are not only environmental but also cultural, affecting Indigenous communities and the broader global context. The advanced ecological studies of Siberia's environment thus provide critical insights into the multifaceted nature of environmental change and the urgent need for comprehensive and effective strategies to address these challenges.

The Yeti and Environmental Sciences: Understanding the Habitat

In the realm of environmental sciences, the study of Siberia's habitat is crucial to understanding the theoretical habitat of the Yeti. Siberia, a vast and ecologically diverse region, is undergoing significant environmental changes due to climate change. These changes are not only affecting the physical landscape but also the socio-political dynamics, particularly impacting Indigenous communities.

Siberia's rapid climate change is characterized by exceptional warming in the north and increasing aridity in the south. This drastic change in climate patterns poses a significant challenge to the region's biodiversity and ecosystems. With Siberia's immense freshwater resources, mineral wealth, and vast biodiversity, these climatic changes can have profound implications on the ecological balance and sustainability of the region.

Political issues also play a pivotal role in the environmental situation of Siberia. Indigenous rights organizations face crackdowns, limiting their ability to advocate for their communities amidst these climatic threats. This political tension intersects with environmental concerns, impacting the preservation of Indigenous cultures closely tied to the Siberian environment.

Russian governmental strategies towards climate change are evolving, yet their effectiveness remains questionable. Despite acknowledging the impacts of climate change, including the increase in forest fires, Russia's climate action plans, such as the development of solar power stations and green hydrogen technology, are deemed "critically insufficient" by the Climate Action Tracker. This rating reflects a significant gap in Russia's efforts to mitigate the environmental impacts.

The energy production scenario in Russia, with only a minor fraction coming from renewable sources, further underscores the challenges in achieving climate goals. Russia's plans to increase nuclear and hydropower production fall short of the global requirements for limiting temperature increase to 1.5 degrees Celsius.

The current environmental changes in Siberia, driven by both natural and anthropogenic factors, provide a complex backdrop for understanding the habitat of mythical creatures like the Yeti. The intersection of rapid climatic changes, political dynamics, and socio-economic factors creates a multifaceted environment that is crucial for researchers to consider when studying the ecological aspects of cryptozoological entities like the Yeti. This comprehensive approach to environmental science highlights the importance of addressing climate change and its far-reaching impacts on diverse ecosystems and cultures in regions like Siberia.

Extreme Environments: Survival of the Yeti

The concept of the Yeti, a creature reputed to inhabit the harsh climates of the Himalayas, brings to the forefront the study of extreme environments and the survival strategies of species adapted to such conditions. In the context of environmental science and cryptozoology, understanding how a creature like the Yeti could survive in extreme conditions involves exploring the adaptations necessary for life in severe climates.

The Himalayan region, characterized by its high altitude, frigid temperatures, and rugged terrain, presents a range of environmental challenges. To survive in such an environment, a creature like the Yeti would need specialized physiological and behavioral adaptations. These might include enhanced thermoregulation to withstand the cold, efficient respiratory systems to cope with low oxygen levels at high altitudes, and physical adaptations like a robust, insulated body, possibly with thick fur, to navigate and endure the demanding landscape.

Moreover, the Yeti's survival would also depend on its ability to find adequate food and shelter in a region where resources are scarce. This implies a high level of adaptability and possibly a diverse diet. The Yeti, as a hypothetical creature, might be omnivorous, feeding on a range of high-altitude flora and fauna, and employing advanced foraging strategies to sustain itself.

Another aspect of survival in extreme environments is the behavioral adaptation. The Yeti, if it were to exist, would likely be a solitary creature or live in small, reclusive groups to reduce competition for limited resources. Its behavior might include nocturnal or crepuscular activity patterns to avoid the harshest weather conditions and potential threats, including human encounters.

The study of the Yeti's potential survival strategies in extreme environments is not just an exercise in cryptozoological speculation but offers valuable insights into the capabilities and limits of animal adaptations. It highlights the remarkable resilience of life and how species evolve over time to thrive in some of the most inhospitable parts of our planet. This exploration also underscores the importance of preserving these fragile ecosystems, which are home to a myriad of known and, perhaps, unknown species.

While the Yeti remains a creature of myth, the environmental sciences provide a framework for understanding the theoretical possibilities of its survival. The study of extreme environments and the adaptations required for survival therein is a fascinating area that bridges the gap between myth and the empirical realities of the natural world.

Explorers' Tales: Early Encounters

In the annals of Yeti lore, early encounters by explorers in the Himalayas and surrounding regions play a pivotal role. These tales, often a blend of personal accounts, local folklore, and hearsay, have significantly shaped the mythos of the Yeti.

The early 20th century marked a surge in Western interest in the Himalayas, with numerous expeditions attempting to conquer these uncharted territories. Among these adventurers, some reported strange footprints and sightings that they attributed to the Yeti. These accounts often described a large, bipedal creature with a thick fur coat, adapting well to the harsh, snowy environment.

One of the most notable encounters was during the British Mount Everest expeditions in the 1920s. The explorers, including the famed

George Mallory, came across large footprints at high altitudes, which local Sherpas identified as belonging to the "Metoh-Kangmi," translated as "man-bear snowman." This incident brought the Yeti to the attention of the Western world, sparking curiosity and skepticism alike.

Another significant account comes from the 1951 Everest Expedition led by Eric Shipton. Shipton captured photographs of large, mysterious footprints in the snow, which he claimed belonged to the Yeti. These images caused a worldwide sensation, further fueling the intrigue and mystery surrounding this elusive creature.

These early explorers' tales, while lacking in scientific rigor, played a crucial role in perpetuating the legend of the Yeti. They bridged the gap between local myths and global fascination, transforming the Yeti from a regional legend into a worldwide phenomenon. These accounts, embroidered with the thrill of exploration and the allure of the unknown, continue to captivate the imagination, inviting both belief and skepticism.

In examining these tales, it is essential to consider the context of the times and the nature of exploration. The early 20th century was an era of discovery and conquest, where the unknown was both feared and revered. The Yeti, in this narrative, emerged as a symbol of the unexplored and the mysterious, a testament to the vast unknown still present in a rapidly shrinking world.

The early encounters of explorers with the Yeti phenomenon represent a fascinating intersection of exploration, folklore, and the human quest for understanding the unknown. These tales, while largely anecdotal, have undeniably contributed to the rich tapestry of Yeti lore and continue to fuel the debate on the existence of this enigmatic creature.

Historical Expeditions: The Quest for the Yeti

The fascination with the Yeti has led to numerous expeditions over the years, aimed at uncovering the truth behind this enigmatic creature. Among the most notable of these is the Silver Hut expedition, led by Sir Edmund Hillary, a famous mountaineer known for his ascent of Mount Everest. This expedition, conducted in the early 1960s, was one of the most comprehensive efforts to find the Yeti.

The expedition was drawn to the Rolwaling Valley in Nepal, known among the Sherpas as "the grave," due to its challenging mountaineering conditions. This location was selected based on the famous 1951 photographs of yeti footprints taken by Eric Shipton during his exploration. These footprints led to numerous theories and speculations about the existence of the Yeti.

The Silver Hut expedition was a significant undertaking, involving 310 Sherpas, 21 scientists, various specialists, and climbers. The team's objectives were multifaceted, including establishing high-altitude huts and studying the effects of high altitude on human physiology, alongside the search for the Yeti. The team discovered a set of footprints on the Ripimu Glacier, which renewed interest in the Yeti. In an attempt to find the creature, they set up traps, including tripwires, tranquilizer-loaded guns, telescopes, cameras, and microphones, at 18,000 feet. Despite their efforts and the advanced technology of the time, the expedition failed to capture any concrete evidence of the Yeti.

In addition to physical searches, the expedition also examined alleged Yeti artifacts collected over the years. These included various animal skins and bones, among them a yeti scalp. Marlin Perkins, director of Chicago's Lincoln Park Zoo and host of "Wild Kingdom," joined the expedition and provided a zoologist's perspective on these artifacts. His expertise in animal biology helped debunk many of the alleged Yeti artifacts, revealing them to be misidentified animal parts.

Perkins addressed the Yeti theory on "Wild Kingdom" in 1963, comparing the Yeti's supposed footprints to those of primates like chimpanzees and gorillas. His analysis demonstrated significant differences, challenging the notion of the Yeti as a primate-like creature.

These historical expeditions, especially the Silver Hut expedition, represent a significant chapter in the story of the Yeti. They reflect the human spirit of exploration and the desire to understand the unknown. While these expeditions did not provide conclusive evidence of the Yeti's existence, they significantly contributed to our understanding of high-altitude environments and the wildlife inhabiting them. The efforts of explorers like Hillary and Perkins underscore the importance of scientific rigor in the study of cryptids like the Yeti.

The Yeti in Historical Encounters: A Detailed Review

The legend of the Yeti, also known as the Abominable Snowman, has been a subject of intrigue and mystery for centuries. Over the years, there have been numerous reported encounters and sightings, contributing to the lore surrounding this elusive creature. These historical encounters offer a fascinating glimpse into human interaction with the unknown and the unexplained.

One of the earliest documented references to the Yeti comes from the writings of James Prinsep in 1832. Prinsep, an English scholar and antiquary, noted stories of a hairy, ape-like creature in the Himalayas, as recounted by local inhabitants. These early accounts set the stage for a long-standing interest in the Yeti within Western exploration narratives.

In the early 20th century, the fascination with the Yeti grew, particularly among mountaineers and explorers venturing into the Himalayas. Among the most notable were the British Mount Everest expeditions in the 1920s. During these expeditions, climbers reported seeing large footprints in the snow, which local Sherpas attributed to the Yeti. The Sherpa community has long held beliefs in the existence of a wild, humanoid creature in the Himalayas, and their accounts have been a significant source of information and lore about the Yeti.

The 1950s marked a pivotal era in Yeti exploration, with several expeditions specifically aimed at finding evidence of its existence. Perhaps the most famous of these was the 1951 expedition led by Eric Shipton, which captured photographs of mysterious footprints on the Menlung Glacier near Everest. These photos sparked global interest and debate, leading to several other expeditions in the subsequent years.

One such expedition was the Daily Mail Snowman Expedition of 1954, which sought to explore the Barun Valley, a region known for its Yeti sightings. The expedition, while failing to find concrete evidence of the Yeti, brought back intriguing stories and further anecdotal evidence of its existence.

In 1959, the World Book Encyclopedia sponsored an expedition led by Sir Edmund Hillary, one of the first two individuals confirmed to reach the summit of Mount Everest. This expedition aimed to collect and analyze physical evidence of the Yeti. Despite extensive efforts, the team concluded that the evidence they found, including scalp-like artifacts from monasteries, could be attributed to known wildlife, particularly the Himalayan brown bear.

These historical encounters and expeditions have played a crucial role in shaping the narrative and scientific inquiry into the Yeti. While none have provided conclusive evidence of its existence, they have underscored the challenges of cryptozoological research and the allure of exploring the unknown. The Yeti remains a symbol of the mysteries that the natural world still holds, captivating the imagination of scientists, adventurers, and the public alike.

The historical encounters with the Yeti represent a fascinating intersection of myth, exploration, and science. They reflect humanity's enduring curiosity about the unknown and the lengths to which we will go to seek answers, even in the face of uncertainty and skepticism.

Analyzing Historical Yeti Expeditions: Methodologies and Findings

Historical expeditions in search of the Yeti have been marked by a variety of methodologies and findings, reflecting the evolving nature of exploration and scientific inquiry. These expeditions, ranging from initial anecdotal explorations to more systematic scientific endeavors, have contributed significantly to our understanding of the Yeti legend, though they have yet to provide conclusive evidence of its existence.

One of the earliest systematic approaches to exploring the Yeti phenomenon was seen in the 1950s and 1960s, a period that witnessed heightened interest in the Yeti, partly due to the burgeoning field of cryptozoology. Expeditions during this time were often multidisciplinary, involving mountaineers, zoologists, anthropologists, and even psychologists, reflecting a holistic approach to the study of this elusive creature.

The methodology of these expeditions varied, ranging from the collection and analysis of physical evidence, such as footprints or alleged Yeti remains, to interviews with local inhabitants and examination of cultural artifacts related to the Yeti. Some expeditions, like the 1954 Daily Mail Snowman Expedition, focused on extensive field surveys in areas with reported Yeti sightings. These expeditions often employed tracking techniques, setting up cameras and traps, and collecting biological samples for analysis.

The 1960s saw one of the most notable expeditions led by Sir Edmund Hillary, supported by the World Book Encyclopedia. This expedition took a more skeptical approach, aiming to debunk the Yeti myths. The team examined various artifacts claimed to be from the Yeti, including scalps and skins preserved in local monasteries. Their findings, however, indicated that these artifacts were from known animal species, such as the Himalayan brown bear and langurs.

Another significant expedition was the American Yeti Expedition of 1970, which used infrared photography and sound equipment to try to capture evidence of the Yeti. While innovative for its time, the expedition did not yield any concrete evidence of the Yeti's existence.

Throughout these explorations, several common challenges emerged. The harsh and inaccessible Himalayan terrain made exploration exceedingly difficult. Moreover, the reliance on anecdotal evidence and local folklore often led to subjective interpretations and inconsistencies in reported sightings and encounters. The lack of a standardized methodology in early expeditions also meant that findings were often difficult to replicate or verify.

In summary, the various expeditions undertaken to uncover the truth behind the Yeti legend have been marked by a combination of enthusiasm, skepticism, and scientific inquiry. While they have significantly contributed to our understanding of Himalayan folklore and the natural history of the region, the existence of the Yeti remains an unresolved question, leaving room for future explorations and studies in the realm of cryptozoology and folklore.

Eyewitness Perspectives: Analyzing Accounts

Eyewitness accounts of the Yeti, spanning across different cultures and regions, form a complex tapestry of personal experiences, cultural narratives, and anecdotal evidence. These accounts, while often lacking scientific rigor, offer a human dimension to the Yeti mythos, enriching our understanding of this legendary creature.

The Himalayan region, home to the Yeti legend, has a rich history of eyewitness accounts. Local inhabitants, especially in Nepal and Tibet, have shared stories passed down through generations. These stories often describe encounters with a large, bipedal creature covered in thick fur, known for its elusiveness and mysterious nature.

One of the most common themes in these accounts is the sighting of large, unidentifiable footprints in the snow. Many mountaineers and explorers, including famous personalities like Edmund Hillary and Tenzing Norgay, have reported such findings. These accounts often describe the footprints as being larger than human ones, with a distinct shape that suggests a large, unknown primate.

Another recurring element in eyewitness testimonies is the visual sighting of the creature itself. Descriptions vary, but the Yeti is commonly portrayed as a towering, ape-like being with a strong build and a shaggy coat of hair. Some accounts also mention a distinct, unpleasant odor associated with these sightings, adding another sensory dimension to the encounters.

The credibility of these eyewitness accounts is a subject of debate. Skeptics argue that such sightings can be attributed to misidentified wildlife, such as bears or langurs, which are native to the Himalayan region. The challenging environmental conditions and the influence of local folklore may also contribute to misinterpretations of natural phenomena.

Despite these critiques, the eyewitness accounts hold cultural significance. They reflect the deep connection between local communities and their natural environment, weaving the Yeti into the fabric of their cultural identity. These stories, while not scientifically validated, offer insights into human psychology and the nature of belief, illustrating how legends and folklore can shape our perception of the world.

In analyzing these accounts, it's important to consider the context in which they were made. The Himalayas are a remote and largely unexplored region, where the boundaries between the known and the unknown are often blurred. This setting creates a fertile ground for the imagination and for legends like the Yeti to thrive.

In conclusion, the eyewitness accounts of the Yeti, though varied and often unverifiable, contribute to the enduring allure of this mythical creature. They provide a window into the human experience of the unknown, capturing our collective fascination with the mysteries that still lie beyond our understanding.

Chapter 4
Yeti Encounter 1 - The Andes Expedition

Ancient Mountains, Modern Mystery

In the towering Andes Mountains of South America, Diego, an experienced mountain guide, found himself embarking on an expedition that would blur the lines between his extensive knowledge of the land and the unknown. Along with a diverse group of hikers from various countries, Diego's journey into the Andes was one that he would recount with a mix of awe and uncertainty.

The group's trek began under the wide, clear skies typical of the Andean mornings. Diego, with his deep familiarity with the mountains, led the hikers through breathtaking landscapes, where the air was thin and the views were panoramic. Among the hikers were Sofia, a biologist from Brazil; Michael, a photographer from Canada; and Elena, a folklore enthusiast from Peru.

Their goal was to traverse a less frequented path, one that Diego knew offered both natural beauty and a challenging trek. As they ascended, Diego shared stories about the Andes' rich history and the diverse cultures that had thrived in its valleys and peaks.

It was during the first day, as they were setting up camp near a serene mountain pass, that they stumbled upon something that would change the course of their expedition. Hidden in the snow, they found a series of large footprints, unlike anything Diego or the hikers had seen before. These footprints were large, deep, and had a distinct pattern that suggested a bipedal creature.

Diego, with years of experience in the Andes, was perplexed. The footprints did not match those of any known wildlife in the region. The hikers, intrigued and slightly unnerved, gathered around, discussing the possibilities. Sofia, with her background in biology, was particularly interested, noting the size and shape of the prints.

That night, as they sat around the campfire, Diego delved deeper into Andean legends, sharing tales of mythical creatures said to roam the mountains. Elena, fascinated by folklore, listened intently, adding insights from her own knowledge of Andean myths.

As they retired to their tents, nestled in the shadow of the towering Andes, the discovery of the unexplained footprints had opened a door to a world of possibilities, some rooted in science, others in legend. Diego, usually the one with answers, found himself pondering the mysteries that even these ancient mountains might still hold.

Echoes of the Past

The second day of their expedition began with the group still contemplating the strange footprints they had encountered. As they continued their trek, the path took them through diverse terrains – from rocky outcrops to areas dense with foliage. The Andes revealed its majestic beauty, captivating the group, yet the enigma of the footprints lingered in their conversations. Diego, with his expertise in guiding, maintained a watchful eye, ensuring their safety while navigating the challenging terrain.

It was in the early afternoon when they made a remarkable discovery. In a secluded area, hidden away from the commonly trodden paths, they found ancient rock paintings. These paintings, faded yet discernible, depicted various scenes of Andean wildlife and daily life of indigenous peoples. Among these depictions, however, was an image that stood out – a large, humanoid figure, towering over the other elements in the painting.

The group gathered around the rock art, struck by its implications. Elena, with her knowledge of folklore, shared her insights, suggesting that the figure might be connected to local legends of a giant creature said to inhabit the Andes. Sofia and Michael examined the paintings, considering the possibility of a yet-undiscovered species or a symbolic representation from the past.

That evening, as they set up camp in a sheltered valley, the group's discussion turned to the intersection of myth and reality. Diego recounted more tales he had heard from locals, stories of mysterious beings and unexplained events in the mountains. The presence of the ancient rock art lent a certain credibility to these tales, blurring the lines between folklore and potential historical encounters.

The night brought an unexpected turn. A series of deep, echoing roars reverberated through the mountains, emanating from different directions. The sounds were unlike any typical animal calls known to the group, leaving them in a state of heightened alertness. Diego, despite his extensive experience, could not identify the source, adding to the intrigue and unease of the moment.

Shadows Amongst the Peaks

On the third day of Diego and his team's expedition in the Andes, the mysterious events of the previous days had cast a palpable shadow over the group's adventure. The morning began with a quiet, reflective atmosphere, as each member processed the echoing roars that had disturbed the stillness of the previous night.

As they resumed their trek, the awe-inspiring beauty of the Andes continued to unfold around them. However, the group's attention was now divided between admiring the natural splendor and seeking answers to the mysteries they had encountered. Diego led the group with a newfound caution, his usual confidence tempered by the unexplained phenomena.

Their path that day took them through a series of narrow passes, flanked by towering peaks that seemed to watch over them. The tranquility of the high-altitude environment was occasionally broken by the distant sound of an avalanche, a stark reminder of the mountain's raw power.

In a particularly remote section of the trail, the group made another startling discovery. Scattered around their campsite, they found several large footprints, distinct from the ones they had seen earlier. These new prints were fresh, suggesting that whatever had made them had been there while they slept.

The group examined the footprints with a mix of curiosity and unease. Diego, though experienced in the ways of the mountain, admitted he had never seen anything like this. Sofia, with her scientific background, was intrigued but baffled. The footprints defied easy classification, not matching any known wildlife in the Andes.

That night, as they huddled around the campfire, the group shared their thoughts and theories. Elena suggested that they might be witnessing evidence of a legend come to life. Michael, ever the skeptic, proposed more rational explanations, though he struggled to fully rationalize their experiences.

The air of mystery deepened when, just before dawn, they briefly glimpsed a large, shadowy figure in the distance. It appeared only for a moment before vanishing into the thickets of the mountain. This sighting, though fleeting, left the group in a state of heightened alertness and wonder.

As they prepared to depart the next morning, the unanswered questions surrounding their experiences loomed large. They had embarked on a trek through the Andes seeking the beauty and challenges of the mountains but found themselves immersed in a story that bridged the gap between the tangible world and the legends that have long echoed amongst these ancient peaks.

Departure with Doubts

The last day of their journey began with a palpable sense of reflection. The group, having witnessed the unexplained footprints and the fleeting glimpse of a mysterious figure, found themselves grappling with a multitude of questions. The serene beauty of the Andes at dawn stood in stark contrast to the enigmatic and somewhat unnerving experiences they had encountered.

As they made their way down the mountain, retracing their steps through the rugged terrain, Diego led with a quiet introspection. The usual stories and legends he shared with trekkers had taken on a new significance in light of their recent experiences. The group moved with a sense of camaraderie, bonded by the shared mystery they had encountered.

Upon their return to civilization, the group found themselves changed by their expedition. The unanswered questions about the footprints and the mysterious figure left them with a lingering sense of wonder and a deeper appreciation for the mysteries of the Andes.

Diego, in recounting the story, expressed a newfound respect for the legends he had grown up with. The experience had taught him that the mountains held secrets far beyond what he had known, bridging the gap between the legends of the past and the experiences of the present.

The expedition had begun as a journey through the physical landscapes of the Andes but had evolved into an exploration of the unknown, a testament to the enduring mysteries that still lie hidden in the mountains' vast expanse.

Chapter 5
Analyzing the Yeti Evidence

Analysis of Testimonies: A Deeper Look

The Yeti, a creature of folklore and myth, has intrigued humanity for centuries. Its existence, debated and explored through various lenses, remains a fascinating subject. This analysis delves into the testimonies and sightings of the Yeti, evaluating their credibility and exploring the intersection of myth and reality.

Iconic Yeti Sightings

The allure of the Yeti has led to numerous expeditions and sightings, each contributing to the enigma surrounding this elusive creature. Among the most notable encounters is the discovery of peculiar tracks by Eric Shipton in 1951 near Mt. Everest, which presented large, human-like impressions in the snow, hinting at a creature of immense size and strength. Similarly, famous mountaineers Reinhold Messner and Peter Habeler in 1986 reported sighting a Yeti, describing it with human-like features and significant physical presence.

In Tibet, in 1888, William Hugh Knight reported seeing a wild man, describing it as under six feet tall, almost naked in the cold, with a pale yellow complexion, matted hair, and formidable hands. Major Bill Tilman, in Northern India in 1937, encountered tracks in the snow he attributed to the Yeti, remarking on their size, depth, and pattern, which led him to speculate about the nature of the creature.

Scientific Analysis of Evidence

Recent scientific endeavors have shed light on the physical evidence attributed to the Yeti. DNA analysis conducted by an international team of scientists on artifacts such as teeth, bone, hair, and mummified skin, believed to be from the Yeti, concluded that these samples belonged to various species of bear native to the Himalayas, including the Asian black bear, the Tibetan brown bear, and the Himalayan brown bear. This revelation, while demystifying some aspects of the Yeti legend, also emphasizes the rich biodiversity of the region and the potential for misidentification of wildlife as mythical creatures.

Moreover, a skull discovered by Sir Edmund Hillary during a 1960 expedition, initially thought to be of the Yeti, was later identified through DNA tests as belonging to a rare species of Tibetan antelope. This finding further illustrates the complexities involved in interpreting physical evidence in the context of mythical creatures.

The Role of Misidentifications and Hoaxes

The history of Yeti sightings is not devoid of misidentifications and hoaxes. In several instances, what were believed to be sightings of the

Yeti turned out to be misinterpretations of natural phenomena or animals common to the region, such as bears or monkeys. Some claims, including a notorious case where two men toured a purported Yeti in the 1950s, were later exposed as fabrications, eroding the credibility of other sightings and fueling skepticism.

The Yeti, a symbol of the unknown and the unexplored, continues to captivate human imagination. While scientific analysis of purported evidence often points to more mundane explanations, the legend of the Yeti endures, fueled by a blend of cultural narratives, historical accounts, and the inherent human desire for mystery. The analysis of testimonies and evidence, though often debunking specific claims, does not diminish the allure of the Yeti but rather enriches our understanding of the complex relationship between myth and reality.

Historical Analysis of Yeti Reports: Evaluating Credibility

The Yeti, a mythic creature of the Himalayas, has been a subject of both awe and scrutiny over the years. Historical analyses of Yeti reports have ranged from accepting them as credible accounts of an unidentified creature to debunking them as misidentifications or fabrications. This chapter delves into the credibility of these reports, drawing upon scientific insights and cultural interpretations.

The Myth and Its Interpretations

The Yeti is deeply ingrained in the Himalayan folklore and belief systems. Indigenous groups such as the Lepcha people view the Yeti as an ape-like glacier spirit influential in hunting success. These cultural narratives often imbue the Yeti with mythical powers and attributes, blurring the lines between physical reality and spiritual belief. For instance, an account by Ang Tsering Sherpa speaks of the Yeti's power to immobilize people before consuming them, demonstrating the intermingling of the real and the mythical in local lore.

The Western Perspective and Scientific Inquiry

Western interest in the Yeti surged in the 20th century, particularly during the 1950s, often termed the 'golden age' of Yeti research. This era saw significant expeditions and discoveries, such as the famous Shipton footprints found by Eric Shipton in 1951 and the Khumjung scalp investigated by Sir Edmund Hillary. These findings, while intriguing, often led to more questions than answers, with some, like the Khumjung scalp, later identified as non-Yeti origins – in this case, as the hide of a serow goat.

Scientific Analysis of Yeti Evidence

Recent advancements in genetics have allowed for a more scientific examination of artifacts attributed to the Yeti. A landmark study conducted DNA analysis on various Yeti-attributed artifacts like teeth, bone, hair, and skin. This study revealed that most of these artifacts were actually from local bear species: the Asian black bear, the Tibetan brown bear, and the Himalayan brown bear. Such findings demonstrate the potential for animal misidentification to fuel the Yeti legend. One exception in the study was a so-called "Yeti" composed of bear hair and dog teeth, further highlighting the complexity and sometimes misleading nature of Yeti evidence.

Impact of Findings on Yeti Beliefs

These scientific revelations, while significant in demystifying certain aspects of the Yeti myth, have not universally diminished belief in the creature. The Yeti continues to hold cultural importance in the Himalayas and remains a subject of fascination worldwide. The scientific community acknowledges the improbability of completely ruling out the existence of cryptids like the Yeti, given the vast unexplored natural world and the continuous discovery of new species.

The evaluation of Yeti reports through historical and scientific lenses presents a complex picture. While many physical evidences attributed to the Yeti have been debunked, the creature's enduring presence in cultural narratives and its symbolic significance remain intact. The intersection of science, folklore, and the human affinity for mystery continues to keep the legend of the Yeti alive, even as empirical evidence challenges its physical existence.

The Science of Tracking: Basic Techniques

In the realm of wildlife research and exploration, tracking is a fundamental skill that merges observation, knowledge, and the art of interpretation. It's a discipline that transcends mere identification of footprints, delving into the behavior, habits, and ecology of animals.

Understanding Animal Movement and Behavior

1. **Routes and Paths**: Animals, like humans, often choose the path of least resistance in their environment. This behavior creates distinct patterns in the landscape, such as trails, runs, and escape routes. Trails are commonly used by various species and are akin to highways in the wild. Runs are less frequently used and may connect specific areas like water sources and feeding spots. Understanding these pathways is crucial for tracking, as they provide insights into animal habits and routines.

2. **Sleeping and Resting Areas**: Identifying areas where animals sleep or rest can yield valuable information. These areas can be beds used consistently, transient beds, or temporary lays used for rest. For instance, a fox may sleep in the open but use a burrow for birthing, while a groundhog's burrow is its permanent residence.

3. **Feeding Zones**: Different species have varied feeding behaviors, which can be deciphered from their feeding areas. Some may feed along trails or runs, while others focus on specific plants or even create patches by eating through vegetation. These feeding patterns can be indicative of the species present in the area.

Signs and Clues

1. **Medium Scale Signs**: These include rubs, hair and feathers, gnaws and chews, scratchings, ground debris, and scat. Each

of these signs can tell a story about the animal's behavior, diet, and even its physical characteristics. For example, the type of gnawing can indicate the animal species, while scat analysis can reveal the animal's diet and health.

2. **Small Scale Signs**: These are subtler and include compressions and disturbances not directly on the ground, like leaf depressions and changes in ground texture. These signs require more careful observation and can provide detailed information about animal movement and behavior.

3. **Applied Sign Tracking**: This involves using various signs, like scrapes on trees, droppings, and feeding signs, to locate and learn about animals. It's about piecing together a comprehensive picture of an animal's life and activities in a given area. For example, a deer rub on a tree could indicate the presence of a male deer during the mating season.

Learning and Mastering Tracking

Learning to track effectively involves consistent practice and observation in the field. This "dirt time" is essential for developing the skills to identify and interpret various signs. Key aspects include:

- **Identifying Tracks**: Recognizing the distinct tracks of different animals, including the size, number of toes, and presence of nails or claws.

- **Asking the Right Questions**: Effective tracking is not just about identifying a track but understanding the story behind it. Questions like what the animal was doing, when it passed by, and its intentions are crucial to deciphering tracks.

- **Adaptability**: Effective tracking can be done in various environments, not just sand or snow. As skills improve, trackers can discern useful information from more challenging substrates.

Importance in Conservation

Tracking is not just an ancient skill; it plays a vital role in modern wildlife conservation. By understanding animal behavior and movement, conservationists can make more informed decisions about habitat protection and management strategies. This skill also preserves indigenous knowledge and enhances observation and critical thinking skills, which are vital for comprehensive ecosystem understanding and management.

Tracking in wildlife research is a complex, nuanced discipline that combines knowledge of animal behavior, ecology, and environmental patterns. Its applications are crucial for conservation efforts, ensuring a deeper understanding of animal habits and their interactions with the ecosystem.

Advanced Tracking Techniques: Modern Methods

In the evolving field of wildlife research, advanced tracking techniques have significantly enhanced our understanding of animal behaviors and ecosystems. These modern methods, combining cutting-edge technology and innovative approaches, offer profound insights into the lives of wildlife, including elusive species like the Yeti, if it exists.

Satellite Imagery and Wildlife Tracking

High-resolution satellite imagery has become an invaluable tool in wildlife monitoring. This technology transcends geographical boundaries and provides vital data on wildlife and their threatened habitats globally. It has been effectively used to detect illegal activities, map coral reefs, monitor desertification and deforestation, and even count large animal populations in remote or inaccessible areas. For instance, scientists have discovered new colonies of emperor penguins by analyzing guano stains on ice through satellite imagery.

Satellite-Based Tracking Tags

Satellite-based tracking tags, such as ARGOS and GPS systems, have revolutionized animal tracking over the past decades. ARGOS, operational since the 1970s, uses tags that transmit location data to polar-orbiting satellites. Initially suitable for larger animals due to the size of the tags and the batteries required, advancements in technology have miniaturized these devices, making them applicable to smaller species like birds. GPS tags, on the other hand, receive data from satellites to determine an animal's location, which can then be transmitted to cellular towers or, in remote areas, back to satellites. These tags can also be equipped with sensors to monitor health, fertility, and environmental conditions.

The ICARUS Initiative

The ICARUS (International Cooperation for Animal Research Using Space) Initiative represents a significant leap in wildlife tracking technology. This Internet of Things system is designed for tracking small flying animals using GPS tags and tiny radio transmitters. Signals from these solar-powered transmitters, which weigh only a few grams, are received by an antenna on the International Space Station. This system allows for a more precise and less invasive tracking of smaller species, and future advancements could make these devices light enough to attach to insects like honeybees or butterflies.

Drones in Wildlife Monitoring

Drones have become an increasingly important tool in wildlife ecology, especially for data collection and population surveys. They offer a more precise and accurate means of counting wildlife populations than traditional methods. Drones are particularly useful for surveying animals in breeding and nesting sites, and their versatility allows them to monitor a wide range of species, from waterbirds to marine creatures like sea turtles and dugongs.

Facial Recognition Technology for Primates

Facial recognition technology, similar to that used in humans, is now being explored to identify individual primates. This advancement allows researchers to address key questions in ecology, behavior, and conservation. For example, researchers at the University of Oxford have trained artificial intelligence using a long-term archive of chimpanzee video footage, enabling accurate individual identification.

Camera Traps and Wildlife Insights

Camera traps are among the most effective methods for monitoring endangered species. A single camera trap can store tens of thousands of wildlife images, providing an unparalleled view of animal behaviors and habitats. Wildlife Insights, a cloud-based platform, houses the largest publicly accessible database of camera trap images in the world. This platform allows researchers to share and analyze wildlife data, using AI-enabled software to quickly process and classify thousands of images, significantly speeding up data analysis.

These advanced tracking techniques represent a blend of traditional ecological knowledge and modern technological innovation. They are crucial for conservation efforts, providing detailed and accurate data that inform strategies to protect wildlife and their habitats. As technology continues to advance, we can expect even more sophisticated and efficient methods for monitoring wildlife, deepening our understanding of the natural world.

The Yeti and Wilderness Survival: Theories and Speculations

The Yeti, a creature woven deeply into Himalayan folklore, represents a fascinating intersection of myth, culture, and the human connection with the wild. Over the years, various interpretations and speculations have emerged, painting a complex picture of this mythical being.

Cultural Perspectives and Mythological Significance

1. **Lepcha Beliefs**: Indigenous to the Himalayan region, the Lepcha people view the Yeti as an ape-like glacier spirit influential in hunting success. It's considered a guardian spirit, playing a significant role in their cultural narratives and rituals. After a successful hunt, parts of the prey are offered to the Yeti, believed to be the god of the hunt, in hopes of pleasing it for future hunting expeditions.

2. **Yeti in Nepali Culture**: In Nepal, the Yeti transcends its origins as a Sherpa legend, becoming a prominent figure in the broader Nepali culture. It symbolizes a connection to the wild past and is integrated into various aspects of daily life, including commercial elements like Yeti Airlines and Yeti-themed merchandise. The Yeti Trail, a trekking route in the Barun Valley, reflects this cultural integration, drawing tourists and locals alike.

3. **Yeti's Place in Art and Reincarnation**: In meditational artworks, the Yeti is often depicted in a unique category, positioned between humans and animals, indicating its perceived capacity for thought and kindness. This portrayal contrasts with the Western view of the Yeti as a monstrous entity, a misconception stemming from a mistranslation of the term "metoh-kangmi" (man-bear snow-man) by journalist Henry Newman in 1921.

The Yeti in Western Exploration and Nazi Expeditions

1. **Western Expeditions**: The Yeti caught the attention of

Western explorers in the 20th century, leading to various scientific expeditions, including those by Sir Edmund Hillary. These expeditions contributed to the Western perception of the Yeti, often diverging from local beliefs and interpretations.

2. **Nazi Interest in the Yeti**: In the 1930s, the Nazis, particularly the Ahnenerbe Society, funded expeditions to the Himalayas, partly in search of the Yeti. They believed remnants of a "Nordic-Atlantic original culture" survived in the Himalayas. While zoologist Ernst Schäfer, who led the expedition, was more interested in the region's zoology, they returned with various artifacts and a Tibetan bear, mistakenly believed by some to be a Yeti.

The Most Credible Yeti Sighting

Eric Shipton, a respected British mountaineer, took what is considered the most credible photograph of a Yeti footprint in 1951. This sharp, large footprint, found on the Menlung Glacier, sparked widespread interest and debate about the Yeti's existence. Shipton's reputation as a seasoned explorer lent credibility to the photograph, fueling long-standing curiosity and fascination with the Yeti.

The Yeti, as a cultural and mythical figure, reflects the diverse interpretations and beliefs of the people in the Himalayan region. While Western perspectives and expeditions have often skewed its image, the Yeti remains a significant part of local folklore, symbolizing the deep connection between humans and the wild. The blend of cultural reverence and scientific curiosity surrounding the Yeti continues to fascinate and inspire people globally.

Forensic Analysis of Evidence: An Examination

The enigma of the Yeti, often referred to as the Abominable Snowman, has captivated human imagination for centuries. While much of the discourse around the Yeti is steeped in folklore and anecdote, the advent of forensic science offers a new lens to examine evidence attributed to this mythical creature. Let's delve into various aspects of forensic analysis related to the Yeti phenomenon.

Hair and Tissue Analysis

One of the most common pieces of evidence claimed to be associated with the Yeti are samples of hair, skin, or tissue. In recent years, forensic analysis of these samples has been conducted to determine their origin. For instance, several studies have analyzed hair samples believed to belong to the Yeti. DNA analysis often reveals that these samples correspond to known wildlife species, particularly bears and other Himalayan fauna. This genetic evidence challenges the notion of the Yeti as an unknown primate species, suggesting instead cases of mistaken identity or folklore misinterpretation.

Footprint Examination

Footprints alleged to belong to the Yeti have been a significant source of both intrigue and controversy. Forensic experts have analyzed photographs and casts of these footprints, often found in remote snow-covered regions of the Himalayas. Detailed examination of these prints, including size, depth, and pattern, has led to various interpretations. Some researchers argue that the footprints could belong to large bears or other known animals, potentially distorted by melting snow. Others maintain that certain characteristics of the prints do not match known wildlife, leaving room for speculation.

Historical Artifact Assessment

Various artifacts, including so-called Yeti skulls or bones, have been subjected to forensic scrutiny. For example, a skull believed to be of the Yeti, found in remote Himalayan monasteries, was analyzed and later identified as that of a goat-like animal. These examinations often utilize radiocarbon dating and DNA testing to ascertain the age and species origin of the artifacts. Such analyses typically demystify the artifacts, attributing them to known animals or human-made objects.

Photographic and Video Evidence

Visual evidence, such as photographs and videos claiming to capture the Yeti, has been critically analyzed using forensic techniques. Experts often assess these visuals for authenticity, signs of tampering, or misinterpretation. Image enhancement and analysis can sometimes debunk these claims, revealing them as hoaxes, cases of mistaken identity, or natural phenomena misinterpreted as the Yeti.

Ethical and Methodological Considerations

In the process of forensic analysis of Yeti evidence, ethical considerations regarding cultural beliefs and traditions are paramount. The Yeti holds significant cultural and spiritual value in Himalayan societies. Therefore, scientists approach the analysis with respect for local traditions and sensibilities. Furthermore, methodological rigor is essential to ensure the validity and reliability of forensic conclusions.

The forensic analysis of Yeti-related evidence plays a critical role in demystifying this legendary creature. While it often challenges the existence of the Yeti as a distinct biological entity, it also enriches our understanding of Himalayan wildlife and biodiversity. The interplay of science and folklore in this context highlights the complex relationship between human belief systems and empirical evidence.

Scientific Analysis of Yeti Evidence: Genetic Testing and More

The scientific quest to unravel the mystery behind the Yeti, a mythical creature of the Himalayas, has led to several groundbreaking studies, particularly in the field of genetics. The analysis of various samples attributed to the Yeti has provided illuminating insights, reshaping our understanding of this legendary being.

Genetic Analysis of Yeti Samples

A significant advancement in Yeti research came with the genetic analysis of samples collected from the Himalayas, believed to be of the Yeti. A comprehensive study, involving the examination of mitochondrial DNA from nine supposed Yeti samples, revealed that most of these samples were from Himalayan or Tibetan brown bears. One sample came from a black bear, and one from a dog. This finding dispels the myth of the Yeti as an unknown primate and links the legend more closely to these bear species, which roam the Himalayan region.

Another interesting aspect of this research was the creation of the first full mitochondrial genomes for the Himalayan brown bear and the Himalayan black bear. This genetic data indicated that the Himalayan brown bear and the Tibetan brown bear are more genetically distinct than previously thought, suggesting a unique evolutionary history for these subspecies.

Misinterpretations and Cultural Influence

The Yeti's portrayal in Western culture has often been influenced by misinterpretations and sensationalism. For instance, the term "Yeti" itself became popular due to a mistranslation by a journalist in the early 20th century. The local term "metoh-kangmi," meaning "man-bear snow-man," was incorrectly translated to "abominable snowman," which significantly altered the creature's image in popular culture.

In Himalayan cultures, the Yeti holds a more nuanced and spiritual significance. Among the Lepcha people, an indigenous group of the Himalayas, the Yeti is seen as an ape-like glacier spirit, a guardian of hunting success. This cultural interpretation contrasts starkly with the monstrous image often portrayed in the West.

Conclusions and Conservation Implications

While the myth of the Yeti as a mysterious primate has been debunked through genetic analysis, the research has brought to light the importance of conservation efforts for Himalayan and Tibetan bears. These bear species, with their unique genetic lineage, are in critical need of scientific attention and conservation measures. The fascination with the Yeti has inadvertently spotlighted the ecological and cultural richness of the Himalayas, emphasizing the need to preserve both its biodiversity and cultural heritage.

In summary, scientific analysis, particularly in genetics, has played a pivotal role in demystifying the Yeti legend. It has not only refuted the existence of an unknown primate but also underscored the significance of Himalayan wildlife and the need for its conservation. The Yeti legend, while rooted in myth, continues to inspire scientific inquiry and cultural interest, bridging the gap between folklore and empirical knowledge.

Genetic Enigmas: A Beginner's Guide

The study of genetics, particularly in the context of cryptids like the Yeti, presents a fascinating intersection between myth and science. This chapter introduces the basics of genetic analysis and how it applies to the study of cryptids, focusing on unraveling the genetic enigmas surrounding the Yeti legend.

Introduction to Genetics in Cryptid Research

Genetic research in cryptid studies involves analyzing DNA from alleged cryptid samples, such as hair, skin, or other biological material. The primary goal is to determine the species origin of these samples. This process involves extracting DNA, amplifying specific regions through polymerase chain reaction (PCR), and then comparing the sequences obtained with known species.

Case Studies in Yeti Genetic Research

1. **The Yeti and Bear Connection**: A pivotal study in Yeti genetics analyzed purported Yeti samples, including hair and bone, using mitochondrial DNA sequencing. The results revealed that most samples attributed to the Yeti were from local bear species, particularly the Himalayan brown bear and the Tibetan brown bear. This study not only debunked some aspects of the Yeti myth but also provided valuable insights into the genetics and evolutionary history of these bear species.

2. **Mitochondrial DNA Analysis**: Mitochondrial DNA (mtDNA) is often used in cryptid genetics due to its abundance in cells and maternal inheritance pattern. MtDNA analysis has proven instrumental in identifying species lineage and divergence times. For instance, the mtDNA analysis in the Yeti study revealed the distinct genetic lineage of the Himalayan brown bear, indicating its ancient separation from other bear populations.

Methodologies in Genetic Cryptid Research

The methodologies used in cryptid genetic research are similar to those in wildlife genetics. They include:

- **DNA Extraction**: Obtaining DNA from biological samples, which can be challenging due to degradation or contamination, especially in field conditions.

- **PCR Amplification**: Amplifying specific DNA regions to obtain sufficient material for sequencing.

- **DNA Sequencing and Comparison**: Sequencing the amplified DNA and comparing it to genetic databases to identify species or genetic relatives.

Ethical Considerations and Cultural Sensitivity

In conducting genetic research on cryptids, it's crucial to approach the subject with cultural sensitivity and ethical considerations. Many cryptids, like the Yeti, are deeply ingrained in local cultures and folklore. Scientists must respect these beliefs while conducting and presenting their research.

Challenges and Future Directions

Genetic research on cryptids faces several challenges, including the scarcity of reliable samples, potential contamination, and the limitations of current genetic technology in identifying unknown species. Future advancements in genetic analysis, such as next-generation sequencing and environmental DNA (eDNA) analysis, could provide more definitive answers and potentially uncover new aspects of cryptid biology.

The application of genetics to the study of cryptids like the Yeti offers a scientific approach to exploring these legends. While often debunking mythical creatures' existence as distinct species, genetic analysis contributes to our understanding of biodiversity and evolutionary biology. It bridges the gap between folklore and science, providing tangible insights into the natural world's mysteries.

Advanced Genetic Theories: In-Depth Analysis

In the realm of cryptid research, particularly concerning the Yeti, advanced genetic theories and analyses have significantly contributed to our understanding. These theories delve deeper into the genetic makeup of samples collected, believed to be associated with cryptids like the Yeti.

Materials and Methods in Cryptid Genetic Research

Cryptid DNA studies typically involve collecting and analyzing hair samples, preferred due to their retention of genetic material. The process of sample submission is rigorous, with steps to eliminate human contamination and ensure authenticity. Techniques like infrared fluorescence examination are used to screen samples for genuine cryptid material.

Genomic Data and Phylogenetic Analysis

Genomic sequence data is crucial in cryptid research, offering a foundation for in-depth molecular studies. Platforms like Gen-Bank are instrumental, allowing researchers to compare sequences with known species. Molecular phylogenetic analyses are employed to trace the evolutionary pathways of potential cryptids, comparing their DNA sequences with known species to ascertain genetic affiliations.

DNA Sequence Analysis and Species Identification

DNA sequence analysis focuses on mitochondrial DNA, especially its hypervariable regions, to discern species differences. These analyses have uncovered sequences suggesting the existence of unknown hominin species and have shown links to known bear species and other mammals, indicating a diversity of wildlife in regions associated with Yeti sightings.

Discoveries and Implications

Genetic analyses have led to the discovery of previously unrecognized bear species, suggesting different evolutionary events. Furthermore, studies on anomalous primate samples have provided insights into morphological convergence among species. These findings have implications for our understanding of biodiversity and human genetics, indicating potential links between modern humans and unknown hominin species.

Challenges and Future Directions

Cryptid DNA studies face challenges like contamination and the limitations of reference sequences. The field requires expanded genomic databases and further research into nuclear DNA analysis, which could unveil more information about cryptids.

Advanced genetic theories in cryptid research, particularly regarding the Yeti, have reshaped our understanding of biodiversity and human evolution. These studies bridge the gap between myth and science, offering insights into the natural world's mysteries and the evolutionary history of species.

The Yeti and Modern Science: DNA, Genetics, and Beyond

The investigation into the Yeti's existence through modern science, particularly in the realms of DNA and genetics, has opened new avenues of understanding. This chapter delves into how contemporary scientific methods are applied to explore the enigmatic Yeti legend.

DNA and Genetic Analysis

1. **DNA Sequencing of Alleged Yeti Samples**: Efforts to sequence DNA from purported Yeti samples, such as hair or tissue, have been instrumental in demystifying the Yeti legend. These genetic analyses often reveal that the samples belong to known wildlife species, particularly Himalayan bears. Such findings indicate the likelihood of misidentification or mythologization of these animals as Yetis.

2. **Genetic Divergence and Bear Species**: Detailed genetic studies have shown significant divergence within bear species in the Himalayas. This divergence is crucial in understanding the region's biodiversity and evolution. The research also sheds light on the genetic uniqueness of the Himalayan brown bear, emphasizing its conservation importance.

Integrating Genetic Data with Ecological Studies

Modern genetic studies are often combined with ecological research to gain a comprehensive understanding of the Himalayan ecosystem. This approach helps in discerning the distribution, behavior, and adaptation strategies of wildlife in extreme environments, which are often attributed to the Yeti.

Limitations and Challenges

While genetic analysis provides clarity, it also faces challenges like sample contamination and the limited range of DNA comparison databases. Addressing these issues requires meticulous sample handling and expanding genetic databases to include a broader spectrum of species.

The Future of Yeti Research

Future research directions may involve more advanced genetic techniques like CRISPR and genome editing, which could uncover further details about the biodiversity of the Himalayas. Additionally, environmental DNA (eDNA) analysis could play a pivotal role in detecting elusive species in the region, possibly providing more concrete answers about the Yeti's existence.

In summary, the integration of modern science, particularly genetics and DNA analysis, into Yeti research has transitioned the field from myth and legend into a domain of scientific inquiry. While the existence of the Yeti as a distinct species remains unproven, these scientific endeavors have greatly enhanced our understanding of the Himalayan ecosystem and its inhabitants.

Chapter 6
Psychological, Sociological and Economic Impact of the Yeti

The Psychology of Belief

In exploring the psychology of belief, particularly in relation to mythical creatures like the Yeti, several fascinating aspects emerge. These beliefs are not mere fantasies; they are deeply intertwined with human psychology and the way our minds process narratives and the unknown.

The Yeti, also known as the "Abominable Snowman," is a prominent figure in cryptozoology, which refers to the study of animals that are claimed to exist but whose existence has not been proven. This field includes creatures like Bigfoot and the Loch Ness Monster, which, like the Yeti, have captivated human imagination for centuries.

Belief in such creatures is often rooted in our psychological make-up. One key aspect is the narrative nature of human cognition. Our brains are wired to remember and interpret information more effectively when it's structured as a story. This narrative construction helps us make sense of the world, and it's deeply ingrained in our psychology. Myths and legends, including those about the Yeti, leverage this aspect by weaving stories that resonate with our experiences and emotions.

These stories often represent a form of reconstructive memory. Memory isn't a literal replaying of events but rather a reconstruction that makes sense of our experiences. When people recount sightings of mythical creatures like the Yeti, they're often influenced by this reconstructive nature of memory, which can lead to embellishments or misinterpretations of their experiences.

The allure of mythical creatures also lies in their representation of the unknown and unexplored aspects of our world. The Yeti, for instance, embodies the mysteries of the remote and uncharted territories it is said to inhabit. It's a symbol of the unexplored and the wild, representing a bridge between the known and the unknown, the civilized and the wild.

Belief in such myths can also be seen as a reflection of the human desire for exploration and discovery. The idea of encountering a creature like the Yeti taps into our innate curiosity and the thrill of exploring the unknown. This can be particularly appealing in an age where scientific and technological advancements have made the world seem smaller and more comprehensible.

The popularity of these beliefs, despite the lack of concrete evidence, indicates a deeper psychological need. In a world increasingly governed by rationality and science, myths offer a counterbalance. They provide a space for imagination and wonder, allowing people to engage with ideas and possibilities that transcend everyday reality.

In the context of the Yeti, the psychological fascination is further compounded by its cultural significance. Originating from the remote regions of the Himalayas, the Yeti is not just a cryptid but a cultural symbol, intertwined with the folklore and traditions of the local communities. This cultural dimension adds layers of meaning and significance to the myth, making it more than just a tale of an elusive creature.

Finally, the belief in mythical creatures like the Yeti also touches upon the broader human experience of dealing with the unknown. Myths and legends serve as a way for people to conceptualize and engage with the mysteries and uncertainties of the world. They provide a framework for understanding and relating to aspects of our environment that are beyond our immediate comprehension.

The psychology of belief in myths like the Yeti reveals a complex interplay of narrative cognition, cultural significance, and the human quest for understanding the unknown. These myths are not just fanciful tales; they are integral to the human experience, offering insights into our psychology and our continuous search for meaning in the world around us.

Psychological Impact of Mythology

The psychological impact of Yeti legends on society is a multifaceted phenomenon that intertwines mythology, psychology, and cultural narratives. The Yeti, often referred to as the "Abominable Snowman," is a mythical being from Himalayan folklore, described as a large, ape-like creature inhabiting remote, snow-covered regions, particularly in Nepal and Tibet. Its mystique and speculation are fueled by reports of footprints, sightings, and local stories.

Mythology, by its nature, is a powerful psychological tool that helps people make sense of the world. Myths serve as a means to express unconscious desires and fears, acting as allegories for deeper human experiences and emotions. In this context, the Yeti can be seen as a representation of the unknown, the unexplored, and perhaps a reflection of humanity's fears and curiosities.

The Yeti's role in different cultures varies significantly. In Himalayan countries, Yetis are often depicted as helpful beings, guiding lost travelers in the mountains and repaying kindness with kindness. They occupy a unique place in the pattern of rebirth and reincarnation, existing in a category between humans and animals, capable of thought and kindness. This contrasts sharply with the Western perception of the Yeti as a monstrous creature, a view that emerged largely due to a translation error in the early 20th century by journalist Henry Newman, who misinterpreted the term "metoh-kangmi" (man-bear snow-man) as "abominable snowman".

The psychological appeal of Yeti legends can be linked to the fundamental human tendency to create and believe in narratives. Human memory and cognition are narrative in nature. We remember and make sense of the world through stories. This reconstructive nature of memory can lead to embellishing or misinterpreting experiences, contributing to the perpetuation of myths like the Yeti. Such myths are not just fanciful tales; they represent a way for people to conceptualize and engage with the mysteries and uncertainties of the world.

In addition to their role in explaining the unexplained, myths like the Yeti legend serve to bind communities together, providing a shared sense of identity and continuity. The ceremonies and traditions derived from these myths remind us of our connection to something larger than ourselves, forming an integral part of the human experience across cultures and generations.

From a psychological perspective, the Yeti myth exemplifies how folklore and legend can impact belief systems and societal norms. It demonstrates the enduring power of mythology in shaping our understanding of the world and ourselves, transcending the boundaries between truth and fiction, science and spirituality. The Yeti legend, with its rich cultural and psychological dimensions, continues to captivate the human imagination, reflecting our ongoing fascination with the unknown and the mysterious aspects of our existence.

Analyzing the psychology of human narratives

The psychological analysis of Yeti sightings, a key aspect of cryptozoology, delves into the realm of belief and perception, unraveling why and how people come to believe in and report sightings of such cryptids.

One intriguing aspect of this phenomenon is the human propensity for constructing and believing in narratives, particularly those that challenge the boundaries of known science. This narrative inclination is deeply embedded in our psychology and can influence how we perceive and interpret unusual or unexplained phenomena. When faced with ambiguous stimuli, such as uncertain tracks or fleeting glimpses in remote areas, the human mind often gravitates towards more fantastical interpretations, like the Yeti, rather than mundane explanations. This tendency is further fueled by cultural narratives and folklore surrounding such creatures.

In the case of the Yeti, cultural influences play a significant role. The Yeti's depiction varies across cultures, from a benevolent guide to travelers in the Himalayas to a fearsome creature in Western interpretations. These cultural narratives can shape the way individuals perceive and report sightings, infusing their interpretations with elements from these stories.

Another significant factor is the role of hoaxes and misinterpretations in perpetuating the myth of the Yeti. Throughout history, there have been instances where supposed evidence of cryptids like the Yeti was later revealed to be hoaxes or misidentifications. For example, in the realm of cryptozoology, famous photographs or sightings have often been debunked as fabrications or mistaken identities of known animals. This aspect highlights the complex interplay between belief, desire for discovery, and the often-misleading nature of purported evidence.

Despite the lack of concrete scientific evidence supporting the existence of the Yeti, the legend persists, fueled by a combination of cultural narratives, psychological predispositions, and the allure of the unknown. The Yeti phenomenon exemplifies the human fascination with exploring the unexplained and the power of myth in shaping our understanding of the world. The psychological analysis of Yeti sightings offers insights not just into the nature of this particular cryptid, but into broader aspects of human cognition, belief, and the enduring appeal of mysteries in our collective consciousness.

Fear, Curiosity, and Belief

The Yeti, often known as the "Abominable Snowman", is a cryptid that has captured human imagination and curiosity, revealing much about our psychological tendencies. The legend of the Yeti is deeply rooted in cultural narratives and psychological factors that influence human belief in such mysterious creatures.

One intriguing aspect of the Yeti's impact on human psychology is its representation as a 'Wild Man', a figure that has appeared in various cultures throughout history. This archetype typically involves a large, hairy being, somewhat human but also distinctly different, often perceived as living on the fringes of civilization and nature. The 'Wild Man' myth reflects our complex relationship with the natural world and our own 'uncivilized' past. In modern times, this myth has evolved and found new expressions in the stories of cryptids like the Yeti and Bigfoot.

The term "Abominable Snowman" itself originated from a translation error by journalist Henry Newman in the 1920s, who misinterpreted the Tibetan term "metoh kangmi", which means "man-like wild creature". This translation captured the public's imagination, particularly in the West, where it was molded into a more monstrous figure than its original cultural context might have suggested. This highlights the role of language and communication in shaping our perceptions of myths and legends.

The enduring fascination with the Yeti also illustrates broader psychological phenomena, such as the human tendency to believe in the unprovable and irrational, even in an age dominated by rational, scientific explanations. This inclination can be seen as a counterbalance to the empirical and materialistic understanding of the world, offering a space for mystery and the exploration of the unknown. The phenomenon of cryptids like the Yeti challenges our concepts of reality and pushes the boundaries of our known world.

Despite the lack of scientific evidence supporting the existence of the Yeti, the legend persists, driven by a combination of cultural narratives, psychological predispositions, and the allure of the unknown. The Yeti myth, therefore, is not just about the search for a cryptid; it's about the human quest for understanding, the thrill of exploration, and the enduring power of myth in shaping our perceptions of the world around us. This makes the study of the Yeti an insightful journey into the realms of psychology, culture, and human belief systems.

Sociological Implications: The Yeti's Impact

The sociological implications of belief in cryptids like the Yeti are multifaceted, encompassing cultural beliefs, social values, religion, and politics. These factors collectively shape how societies view and interpret the existence of such mythical creatures.

Perception plays a crucial role in cryptozoology, influencing how people interpret and believe in creatures like the Yeti. This perception is molded by a myriad of factors including cultural beliefs, myths, legends, personal experiences, and media representations. In the Himalayan region, where the myth of the Yeti has been passed down for generations, local people report sightings and encounters, contributing to the belief in its existence. This contrasts with contemporary societies where belief in such creatures may be viewed as folklore-driven or laughable. However, there's a paradoxical increase in interest and belief in the Yeti in modern society, possibly fueled by social media and the internet's accessibility. This demonstrates how societal beliefs and values can influence perception in cryptozoology.

Religion also significantly influences perceptions in cryptozoology. In various cultures worldwide, religious and mythological narratives often include creatures thought to inhabit the natural world, impacting how these creatures are perceived across generations. For example, in Hindu mythology, creatures akin to the Yeti are viewed as divine, whereas in Western Catholicism, they are often seen as demonic. This indicates that perceptions of mythical creatures are shaped by the religious beliefs and values prevalent in a society.

Political factors, such as scientific research limitations and exploration restrictions, can also shape our perception of cryptids like the Yeti. For instance, political factors like border restrictions and conflicts have historically limited research and exploration in the Himalayan region, influencing our understanding and perception of the Yeti.

Furthermore, the socio-cultural view of cryptozoology suggests that rather than observing a biological phenomenon, we're witnessing a psychological and cultural one, shaped by eyewitness performances, data recall, and cultural settings. This view contrasts with the 'flesh and blood' perspective of cryptozoology, which focuses on proving the physical existence of such creatures. The field of cryptozoology is also influenced by speculative zoology, where cryptids are imagined in detail as radically novel members of their respective groups, often based on assumptions and speculations rather than empirical evidence.

The sociological implications of belief in the Yeti and similar cryptids are deeply rooted in cultural, societal, religious, and political contexts. These factors shape perceptions and beliefs, influencing how societies interpret and react to evidence supporting the existence of these mythical creatures. While the lack of scientific evidence often challenges these beliefs, the cultural and societal significance of such myths continues to captivate human interest and imagination.

Environmental Conservation: The Yeti's Role

The exploration of cryptids like the Yeti can positively impact environmental conservation. This area of study, known as cryptozoology, has historical ties to conservation efforts. For example, Peter Scott, the founder of the World Wildlife Fund, showed interest in the Loch Ness Monster and sought to protect such undiscovered species through conservation laws. The discovery of previously unknown species, such as Homo floresiensis, has highlighted the potential for undiscovered biodiversity. These efforts can promote conservation by fueling public interest and awareness about the natural world and its mysteries. Furthermore, cryptozoology's focus on large, mythical creatures can complement conventional conservation efforts by bringing attention to less-known, plausible species. This synergy between the fascination with cryptids and conservation can foster a deeper appreciation and commitment to preserving biodiversity.

The Influence of Climate Change on the Yeti Myth

Climate change, a global phenomenon, has far-reaching implications that extend even into the realms of mythology and cryptozoology. Let's delve into the potential impact of climate change on legends like the Yeti. As environments transform, especially in regions like the Himalayas, the habitats associated with these mythical creatures are altered. This alteration could hypothetically affect the behaviors and supposed sightings of cryptids like the Yeti.

For instance, melting glaciers and changing forest landscapes could lead to migration of wildlife, thereby possibly increasing the likelihood of encountering unknown species or inspiring new legends. Furthermore, as the natural habitats of known species adjust to climate change, the boundary between the known and mythical could blur, providing fertile ground for the evolution of existing myths or the birth of new ones.

Moreover, climate change raises questions about biodiversity and the survival of species in changing habitats, bringing to the fore the importance of conservation efforts. This aspect is particularly relevant in the context of the Yeti myth, which is deeply rooted in the ecology of the Himalayas. The intersection of environmental science, folklore, and cryptozoology in the context of climate change offers a unique perspective on our understanding of myths and their connection to the natural world.

While the Yeti remains a figure of legend, the impact of climate change on its mythos reflects broader concerns about environmental transformations and their cultural implications. As we witness drastic shifts in global climates, the narratives around mythical creatures like the Yeti may also undergo significant changes, underscoring the deep connection between human culture and the natural environment.

Environmental Impacts on Legends

Climate change, a defining challenge of our times, not only reshapes our physical world but also has the potential to transform our mythologies, like that of the Yeti. Let's delve into how environmental shifts, particularly in the Himalayas, could influence the legend of the Yeti, a creature deeply rooted in the lore of these regions.

Altering Habitats and Mythical Creatures

The Himalayas, a crucial setting for the Yeti legend, are experiencing significant environmental changes due to global warming. Glaciers are retreating, and alpine ecosystems are undergoing rapid transformations. Such ecological shifts might hypothetically influence the narrative of the Yeti. If these cryptids were to exist, their migration patterns, behaviors, and potential interactions with humans could change. This could lead to increased sightings or new interpretations of the Yeti myth, potentially altering its characteristics and narratives in local folklore.

Cultural Reflections of Ecological Changes

Climate change not only impacts the physical environment but also reflects in the cultural fabric of societies. The Yeti, as part of Himalayan folklore, is intertwined with the region's ecological consciousness. As the local environment transforms, so might the cultural expressions and stories, including the Yeti legend. This could manifest in new versions of the myth, adapting to the changing landscapes and perhaps incorporating elements of ecological distress or the shifting balance of nature.

The Yeti as a Symbol in the Climate Dialogue

In the broader context of environmental conservation, the Yeti can be seen as a symbol. It represents the unknown and unexplored aspects of our natural world, many of which are under threat due to climate change. The evolving legend of the Yeti in the context of environmental degradation could serve as a narrative tool to highlight the urgency of addressing climate change and preserving natural habitats.

Scientific Perspective and Mythological Adaptations

From a scientific standpoint, the study of the Yeti legend in the context of climate change offers insights into how myths adapt to environmental realities. As species migrate to new habitats and ecosystems alter, it's conceivable that local populations may report different wildlife encounters, potentially giving rise to new cryptid sightings or reinforcing existing legends like that of the Yeti. These interactions provide a fascinating intersection of zoology, environmental science, and folklore.

The Yeti legend, in the face of climate change, stands at the crossroads of mythology and environmental science. As we witness drastic ecological transformations in the Himalayas, the narratives surrounding the Yeti may evolve, mirroring these changes. This interplay between legend and landscape highlights the profound connection between our cultural myths and the natural world. The Yeti, as a mythical entity, thus becomes a lens through which we can view the impacts of climate change on both our physical and cultural landscapes.

The Yeti in Local Economies - Economic Impact

The legend of the Yeti, a creature deeply entrenched in the folklore of the Himalayas and beyond, has fascinating implications on local economies. Let's examine the economic impact of the Yeti legend, exploring its role in tourism, cultural commerce, and its broader influence on the regional economies of areas where the legend is prevalent.

Tourism and the Yeti Legend

The myth of the Yeti is a significant draw for tourists in regions like Nepal, Bhutan, and parts of India. This fascination fuels a tourism industry based on Yeti-themed treks, expeditions, and cultural tours. These activities not only generate income but also create employment opportunities in remote mountainous regions where economic opportunities are often scarce. The Yeti's allure thus contributes to the local economy by bringing in international and domestic tourists who spend on lodging, food, guides, and souvenirs.

Cultural Commerce and the Yeti

The Yeti myth has given rise to a range of cultural products, from handicrafts and artwork to literature and film. Local artisans and businesses capitalize on the Yeti's popularity, creating and selling Yeti-themed merchandise. This cultural commerce extends beyond physical products to include festivals, exhibitions, and events celebrating the Yeti myth, further stimulating local economic activities.

Conservation Efforts and the Yeti

In some regions, the Yeti myth has been leveraged to promote environmental conservation efforts. By linking the preservation of natural habitats to the legend of the Yeti, conservation organizations have found a unique way to engage local communities and tourists in environmental protection initiatives. This approach has the dual benefit of conserving biodiversity and sustaining eco-tourism, which is a significant source of revenue for these regions.

The Yeti in Modern Marketing and Media

Modern marketing strategies and media have amplified the Yeti's presence in popular culture, influencing a range of industries from adventure tourism to entertainment. Documentaries, books, and films about the Yeti attract global attention, indirectly promoting the regions associated with the legend. This has led to increased interest in these areas, boosting tourism and related economic activities.

The Yeti, a figure of myth and legend, has a tangible impact on the economies of regions where the myth is prominent. Its influence on tourism, cultural commerce, conservation, and media illustrates the multifaceted ways in which a legend can contribute to and shape the economic landscape. This impact underscores the interconnection between cultural narratives and economic development, highlighting the power of mythology in influencing real-world economies.

Chapter 7
Yeti Encounter 2 - The Slopes of Everest

The Ascent into Mystery

The story of Ethan Carter, a seasoned mountaineer and environmental scientist, begins with an expedition that was unlike any he had undertaken before. Ethan, who had spent years exploring and studying the various facets of Mount Everest, was always drawn to the mountain's inexplicable allure and the countless stories it harbored.

In the spring of 2022, Ethan embarked on an expedition to study the impact of climate change on the higher altitudes of Everest. His team consisted of fellow scientists Lara and Raj, alongside Sherpa guide Sonam, a man deeply rooted in the local culture and knowledgeable about the mountain's many legends, including that of the Yeti.

Their journey began in the bustling town of Lukla, a gateway to the Everest region, where the air buzzed with the excitement of trekkers and climbers. Ethan described the initial part of the trek as familiar, a path he had traversed many times, yet always with a sense of reverence for the mountain's unpredictable nature.

As they ascended, the landscape transformed from lush green valleys to the stark, rugged terrain of the higher altitudes. Ethan's focus was on collecting environmental data, but he was also keenly aware of the mountain's history and the mysteries it held.

It was upon reaching a remote campsite, situated above the treeline and surrounded by towering peaks, that their expedition took an unexpected turn. While setting up camp, Lara discovered a series of large, unusual footprints in the snow, distinct from those of any known animal in the region. The footprints were deep, indicating a considerable weight, and had a pattern that suggested a bipedal creature.

Ethan, a man of science, was initially skeptical, attributing the footprints to a possible combination of environmental factors and the high-altitude conditions. However, Sonam's reaction was one of quiet concern; he shared with the team the local lore of the Yeti, often described as a guardian of the high mountains, revered and feared in equal measure.

The discovery of the footprints shifted the focus of their expedition. Ethan, Lara, and Raj, driven by a blend of scientific curiosity and the human fascination with the unknown, decided to document and study the footprints further. The team spent the day following the trail, which led them across a challenging terrain of snowfields and moraines.

As the sun set behind the imposing peaks, casting long shadows over the snow, the team gathered in their tent, sharing their thoughts on the day's findings. Ethan recalled the sense of intrigue and joviality that enveloped the team, a mixture of scientific excitement and the fanciful allure of an age-old mystery.

The Trail of Shadows

The team, now deeply engaged in this unforeseen quest, continued their journey across the rugged terrain, following the trail left by the mysterious creature. The morning broke with a crisp clarity, the sun casting a harsh light on the snow-clad landscape. As they progressed, the footprints led them across a narrow ridge, offering a panoramic view of the Himalayan expanse. Ethan, with his scientific background, meticulously documented each footprint, noting their size, depth, and the stride pattern, all of which suggested a creature of significant size and an upright stance.

Lara and Raj, both seasoned in high-altitude expeditions, shared Ethan's mix of skepticism and fascination. They discussed various possibilities – could these be the imprints of an unknown species of bear, or perhaps the result of a peculiar natural phenomenon? Yet, Sonam's input, grounded in the local lore, continuously echoed the mystical – tales of the Yeti, a creature spoken of in hushed tones by the Sherpa community.

As the day wore on, the trail led them to a secluded valley, surrounded by towering peaks. It was here that the team encountered an unexpected and unsettling sight – a series of crude, yet deliberate, rock formations. These formations, arranged in what appeared to be a purposeful pattern, were unlike anything the team had encountered in their previous expeditions.

Ethan described the moment as a turning point, where the lines between their scientific objectives and the unfolding mystery began to blur. The team carefully examined the area, documenting the rock formations, which seemed to hold a significance that was not immediately apparent.

That evening, as they set up camp in the shadow of an imposing cliff face, the atmosphere among the team was one of contemplative silence. The day's discoveries had deepened the mystery, challenging their understanding of the natural world. Sonam, usually reserved, shared more about the Yeti – stories of encounters passed down through generations, descriptions of a creature that was part of the mountains, both feared and revered.

Ethan lay awake in his tent, pondering the day's events. The footprints, the rock formations, Sonam's tales – all seemed to weave into a narrative that was as old as the mountains themselves.

The following morning, the team awoke to find the landscape transformed. A light snowfall had covered the ground, erasing the trail they had been following. They were now treading a path that lay somewhere between science and legend, each step taking them deeper into the unknown realms of Everest.

The Unseen Observer

The fresh snowfall had blanketed the landscape, transforming it into a pristine, unmarked canvas. The team's initial disappointment at losing the trail was quickly replaced by a sense of awe at the mountain's ever-changing facade.

As they trekked through the fresh snow, Ethan recounted the heightened alertness of the team. Every sound seemed amplified in the stillness – the crunch of snow under their boots, the distant caw of a raven. The vastness of Everest, coupled with the day's uncertainties, instilled a feeling of being mere specks in an ancient, indifferent world.

Midday brought a surreal experience that Ethan described with a mixture of skepticism and wonder. While traversing a steep incline, Lara, who was leading at the time, stopped abruptly. She gestured to the others to be silent and pointed to a ridge a few hundred meters away. There, outlined against the stark whiteness, was a large, humanoid figure, standing motionless, seemingly observing them. Before anyone could react or capture the moment on camera, the figure retreated, disappearing behind the ridge.

The incident sparked a flurry of conversation. Ethan, a scientist, struggled to rationalize the sighting. Was it another climber, a trick of the light, or something else? Sonam, however, was unwavering in his belief – they had seen the Yeti, the guardian of the mountains. His conviction stirred a mixture of emotions in the team – from Lara's excitement to Raj's skepticism.

The rest of the day was spent reaching a more secure campsite, as the weather began to turn. Ethan described the mood that evening as introspective. The sighting had a profound effect on them, raising questions about the nature of their expedition. Was it purely scientific, or had they ventured into something deeper, something that tread the line between the known and the mythical?

That night, the howling wind and the occasional sound of shifting snow seemed to take on new meanings. Ethan lay in his tent, his mind replaying the day's events. The figure on the ridge, the fleeting glimpse they had all shared, had become more than just a visual experience; it was a challenge to their understanding of the natural world.

As dawn broke the next morning, with a clear blue sky and a calm breeze, the team prepared to move on. The sighting from the previous day had changed something fundamental in their expedition. They were no longer just researchers and mountaineers; they had become part of Everest's timeless narrative, a story that continued to unfold in the vast, silent expanses of the snow and rock.

The Mountain's Secret

The team had awoken to a serene morning, the mountain basked in a gentle light, its daunting presence a stark contrast to the tranquility of the dawn. As they continued their descent, the encounter from the previous day was at the forefront of their discussions. Ethan, a man deeply rooted in empirical evidence, found himself grappling with the experience. It was a moment that defied scientific explanation, yet was as real as the snow beneath their feet.

Lara and Raj engaged in heated debates, weighing the possibilities of optical illusions against the stark reality of what they had seen. Sonam, however, remained quiet, his demeanor suggesting a deep understanding, or perhaps acceptance, of the mountain's mysteries.

The day's trek was uneventful in comparison, yet the atmosphere within the group was charged with an unspoken understanding. They had shared an experience that would forever alter their perception of the mountain and its legends.

In the late afternoon, as they neared the end of their journey, the team discovered something that added yet another layer to their expedition's narrative. Partially buried in the snow, they found an old, tattered piece of cloth. Ethan described it as resembling a traditional Sherpa garment, aged and weathered by time and the elements.

The discovery sparked a series of hypotheses. Could it be a remnant from a past expedition, or something more? Sonam examined it and shared a local tale of a Sherpa who had gone missing in the mountains years ago, believed by some to have been taken by the Yeti.

The team's return to Lukla was marked by a sense of accomplishment intertwined with deep introspection. They had set out to study environmental changes but had stumbled upon something that transcended their original mission.

Ethan concluded his account by expressing a newfound respect for the legends and mysteries of Everest. The experience had taught him that some aspects of our world defy conventional understanding, residing in the realm of the unexplained.

The team left the mountain with more questions than answers, their minds teeming with the possibilities of what they had encountered. The footprints, the sighting, the rock formations, and the piece of cloth – each element contributed to a story that was as enigmatic as Everest itself.

In the end, Ethan and his team's experience on the mountain became a testament to the vast, untapped mysteries of our natural world. It was a reminder that, despite our advancements and understanding, there remain phenomena that elude explanation, residing in the shadowy realms between myth and reality.

Chapter 8
The Yeti in Global Media - A Study of Representation

The Yeti, a figure shrouded in myth and mystery, has captivated global media, influencing various forms of representation across cultures. This chapter delves into the portrayal of the Yeti in different media formats, exploring its impact on public perception and the cultural significance of this enigmatic creature.

Global Media and the Yeti Mythos

The global media's fascination with the Yeti transcends geographical and cultural boundaries. From documentaries and news reports to movies and literature, the Yeti has been a subject of intrigue and speculation. These representations often blend fact with fiction, creating a tapestry of narratives that both mystify and attempt to demystify the creature.

Film and Television's Portrayal of the Yeti

In film and television, the Yeti is often depicted in varying lights - from a fearsome beast to a misunderstood creature. This portrayal reflects society's mixed feelings about the unknown and the unexplored. Films and TV shows set in exotic locations often use the Yeti as a plot device to explore themes of adventure, mystery, and the clash between civilization and the wild.

Literary Interpretations of the Yeti

In literature, the Yeti has been a subject of both serious inquiry and imaginative exploration. Books ranging from scientific treatises to children's stories have portrayed the Yeti in multiple dimensions, each contributing to the myth's evolution. This literary representation plays a crucial role in shaping public understanding and attitudes towards the Yeti.

The Yeti in Online and Digital Media

With the advent of the internet and digital media, the Yeti myth has found new life. Online forums, blogs, and social media platforms have become hotbeds for sharing Yeti-related information, sightings, and theories. This digital age has democratized information about the Yeti, allowing more people to engage with the myth, share experiences, and contribute to its global narrative.

The Yeti's representation in global media is a reflection of humanity's enduring fascination with the unknown. Through various forms of media, the Yeti myth continues to evolve, capturing the imagination of people worldwide.

The Yeti in Media: A Basic Overview

The representation of the Yeti in media is a fascinating amalgamation of cultural mythology, scientific inquiry, and popular imagination. The Yeti, often depicted in Western media as a creature with white fur, likely owes this portrayal to its association with its snowy habitat, rather than any grounding in sighting reports which often describe it with reddish-brown coloration. This depiction reflects a broader trend in the portrayal of the Yeti in popular culture, where it is consistently presented in ways that diverge significantly from the original folklore and witness accounts.

The Yeti's journey through the media landscape is not just a tale of misrepresentation but also one of scientific intrigue and cultural misunderstanding. Scientific interest in the Yeti, particularly in the field of genetics, has sought to unravel the truth behind the myriad of physical specimens attributed to this mythical creature. Studies conducted in the 21st century have largely debunked the existence of the Yeti as a distinct species, attributing most of the analyzed specimens to known animals like bears and dogs. This shift in scientific understanding, however, does not diminish the cultural and mythical significance of the Yeti, especially in the Himalayan region where it originated.

In the Himalayas, the Yeti is more than just a mysterious creature; it is an integral part of a rich tapestry of folklore and spiritual beliefs. The Yeti, or 'glacier spirit', is deeply woven into the narratives of local cultures, often embodying more than just a physical entity. It is seen as a spiritual being with a significant role in local mythology, influencing various aspects of life, such as hunting success. This cultural dimension of the Yeti narrative highlights a significant gap in understanding between the Western perception of the Yeti as a cryptozoological curiosity and its original cultural context, which is infused with spiritual and mythological significance.

The Yeti's portrayal in media, therefore, serves as a lens through which we can observe the complex interplay between science, culture, and popular imagination. While the scientific community may have reached a consensus on the biological origins of the Yeti legend, its cultural and mythical significance continues to captivate the imagination of people around the world. The media representation of the Yeti, while often diverging from its original cultural roots, plays a crucial role in keeping this legendary creature alive in the global consciousness, transcending its origins to become a symbol of the mysterious and the unknown.

Global Fascination: Yeti in International Media

The Yeti, a mythical creature often depicted as a large, ape-like being, has captivated audiences and stirred curiosity across the globe. This chapter delves into the phenomenon of the Yeti in international media, exploring the diverse ways in which this enigmatic creature has been represented and discussed across different cultures and media outlets.

The Yeti's Media Coverage Across the World

International media's interest in the Yeti has varied, often influenced by cultural perceptions and scientific discoveries. A notable instance was the widespread coverage of the Indian Army's claim of discovering Yeti footprints in the Himalayas in 2019. This claim attracted global attention, prompting a range of responses from skepticism to intrigue. Media outlets in Japan, Australia, China, Russia, West Asia, the UK, and the US reported on this event, each bringing their unique perspective to the story. While some media outlets focused on the mythological aspects of the Yeti, others approached the story with a scientific angle, debating the credibility of such claims.

This incident is a microcosm of the Yeti's presence in international media - a blend of myth, mystery, and scientific curiosity. The Yeti's portrayal varies significantly across different cultures and nations, reflecting the diverse ways in which the legend is perceived globally.

Scientific Investigations and Media Interpretations

The Yeti's existence has been a subject of scientific interest, particularly in the field of genetics. Studies aimed at uncovering the truth behind Yeti sightings have often found that purported Yeti specimens were in fact from known animal species, primarily bears. This scientific angle has been a crucial aspect of the Yeti's portrayal in the media. For instance, research led by Tianying Lan of the University at Buffalo analyzed 24 samples from the Tibetan Plateau-Himalaya region, which were thought to be from the Yeti. The study found that all samples, except one from a museum exhibit, were from local bear species. This revelation, while demystifying the legend to some extent, also highlighted the importance of the region's biodiversity and the evolutionary history of local bear species.

The media's coverage of such scientific findings plays a significant role in shaping public perception of the Yeti. While it often moves the narrative away from the realm of mythology towards scientific explanation, the allure of the Yeti as a mysterious creature persists in popular culture.

The Yeti's representation in international media is a complex interplay of cultural myths, scientific inquiry, and public fascination. While scientific studies continue to demystify the legend, the Yeti remains a symbol of the unknown, capturing the imagination of people worldwide.

Media Analysis: The Yeti Phenomenon

Scientific Misunderstandings and Cultural Context

The Yeti, often perceived as a cryptozoological phenomenon akin to the Loch Ness Monster, is deeply rooted in the lore of local cultures, especially in the Himalayan region. This mystical creature, often depicted as an ape-like glacier spirit, has been a significant part of local folklore and spirituality, influencing various aspects of life including hunting success. In these cultures, the Yeti transcends the boundary between the real and the supernatural, being both a physical entity and a mythical power. Western interpretations, however, have frequently overlooked this cultural context, leading to a gap in understanding between the original myth and the Western portrayal of the Yeti.

The Yeti in Scientific Inquiry and Popular Culture

Scientific investigations into the Yeti phenomenon have often demythified the legends, with many studies revealing that the supposed evidence of the Yeti, such as footprints or fur samples, belonged to other local species, particularly bears. This scientific scrutiny, while challenging the existence of the Yeti as a distinct species, has also heightened the mystery and allure surrounding it.

In popular culture, the Yeti has evolved from a fearsome beast into an icon of intrigue and mystery. Its depiction in movies, animations, and literature has added a new layer to the mythos, transforming the Yeti into a source of inspiration across various mediums, including technology and art. The Yeti's representation in popular culture signifies a shift in public perception, making it an intriguing figure rather than a fearsome one.

The Yeti Yonder: Influence on Contemporary Society and Culture

The concept of the Yeti extends beyond mere folklore and has a powerful influence in today's society and culture. It finds expression in various forms, from avant-garde music and abstract paintings to gripping novels and high-tech products. Yeti-themed attractions have also become popular, turning remote locations into bustling tourism hotspots. This demonstrates the Yeti's potent influence in shaping cultural and communal narratives.

Psychological Dimensions of the Yeti Phenomenon

The fascination with the Yeti reflects a deep-seated human interest in the extraordinary and the unexplainable. This fascination feeds into a broader matrix of belief systems, with some viewing the Yeti as a spiritual guardian and others enjoying the thrill of delving into these mysteries. The psychological impact of the Yeti phenomenon is significant, as it taps into our innate curiosity and our desire to explore the unknown.

Embracing the Enigma: The Future of the Yeti Phenomenon

As we advance in our understanding of the world, the enigma surrounding the Yeti is likely to evolve rather than diminish. The possibility of future encounters with the Yeti, whether real or mythical, adds to its allure. The exploration of the Yeti phenomenon has broadened our perspective, turning it from a symbol of fear and superstition into a meta-concept that plays with human curiosity and our relentless pursuit of the unknown. The Yeti phenomenon stands as a testament to our insatiable curiosity and our need to connect with the strange and extraordinary.

The Yeti phenomenon is a complex interplay of science, culture, and psychology. It encapsulates our fascination with the unknown and our continual quest to understand the mysteries of our world. The Yeti, as a cultural and mythical figure, continues to captivate and inspire, reminding us of the beauty and allure of the world's unsolved mysteries.

The Yeti in Modern Media: Public Perception and Influence

The Yeti, a legendary creature said to inhabit the Himalayan region, has long been a subject of fascination in both scientific and popular culture. Its representation in modern media has significantly influenced public perception, evolving from a mysterious beast to an icon of popular imagination.

The Yeti's Scientific and Cultural Journey

Initially, the Yeti was considered a possible undiscovered hominid, leading to various scientific explorations and genetic analyses. Studies, particularly those published in the Proceedings of the Royal Society B, have concluded that most physical Yeti specimens, like hair or bones, actually belong to known animals, primarily bears. Despite these scientific findings, the cultural significance and mythological aspects of the Yeti have continued to thrive, indicating a gap between scientific understanding and public fascination.

The Yeti in Popular Culture

In popular culture, the Yeti has been a versatile figure, depicted in various forms ranging from fearsome monsters to friendly beings. Its first major appearance in cinema was in the 1954 film "The Snow Creature," and since then, it has been featured in numerous movies, often reflecting the dual nature of its portrayal. Iconic franchises like Star Wars and Indiana Jones have included Yeti-like creatures, showcasing its widespread influence. This dichotomous representation highlights the Yeti's enduring appeal in the realm of fantasy and adventure.

Perception's Role in the Yeti Phenomenon

The role of perception in cryptozoology is crucial in understanding the public's belief in the Yeti. Cultural beliefs, myths, media representations, and personal experiences significantly shape this perception. The Yeti's myth has been perpetuated through generations in the Himalayan region, with modern media playing a key role in popularizing it. Films, documentaries, and social media have contributed to a renewed interest in the Yeti, transitioning from mere folklore to a subject of genuine curiosity and exploration. This shift in perception, influenced by societal, religious, and political factors, underscores the complex relationship between myth and reality in the context of cryptozoological creatures.

The Yeti: From Fear to Fascination

The transformation of the Yeti in public perception from a symbol of fear to a figure of intrigue reflects a broader cultural shift. The Yeti now embodies the human desire for exploration and the unknown, transcending its origins as a mere cryptid to become a symbol of mystery and adventure. This evolution in perception highlights the power of media and popular culture in shaping and sustaining legends, regardless of their scientific plausibility.

The Yeti's journey through modern media has been a fascinating one, where scientific skepticism intersects with cultural fascination. While the scientific community may have debunked the physical existence of the Yeti, its symbolic presence continues to captivate the public imagination, showcasing the enduring power of myth and legend in our collective consciousness.

The Yeti in the Digital Age: Media and Technology

In the digital era, the mythos of the Yeti has been reshaped and expanded by the pervasive influence of media and technology. This chapter delves into the transformation of the Yeti from a cryptic legend to a cultural icon in the digital world.

The Digital Transformation of the Yeti Legend

The emergence of digital media has dramatically altered how legends like the Yeti are perceived and disseminated. With the advent of the internet, information about the Yeti has become more accessible than ever before. Websites, online forums, and social media platforms have facilitated the exchange of stories, sightings, and theories, contributing to a global conversation about this elusive creature. This digital proliferation has not only kept the legend alive but has also allowed it to evolve with new narratives and interpretations.

The Yeti in Online Communities and Social Media

Online communities dedicated to cryptozoology and the Yeti have become hubs for enthusiasts and skeptics alike. These platforms offer a space for sharing personal experiences, discussing scientific theories, and exploring the folklore surrounding the Yeti. Social media, with its vast reach and immediacy, has played a pivotal role in popularizing the Yeti myth. Viral posts, hashtags, and online campaigns have helped in keeping the Yeti a topic of contemporary relevance, often sparking renewed interest in the legend.

The Impact of Technology on Yeti Research

Advancements in technology have significantly influenced the pursuit of the Yeti. Satellite imagery, advanced camera traps, and environmental DNA (eDNA) analysis have opened new avenues for exploration and research. While these technologies have not provided conclusive evidence of the Yeti's existence, they have reinvigorated scientific interest in the legend and offered novel methods for investigating remote and inaccessible regions of the Himalayas.

The Yeti in Digital Entertainment and Virtual Reality

The Yeti's presence is not limited to online discourse and scientific exploration. In the realm of digital entertainment, video games, virtual reality experiences, and augmented reality apps have integrated the Yeti into interactive narratives. These digital recreations offer immersive experiences, allowing users to engage with the Yeti legend in novel and creative ways. From hunting the Yeti in a video game to virtual expeditions in the Himalayas, technology has enabled a more participatory and dynamic interaction with the legend.

The digital age has transformed the Yeti from a mysterious legend into a multifaceted cultural phenomenon. The proliferation of digital media has ensured that the Yeti legend continues to capture the public's imagination, while advancements in technology have fueled ongoing scientific inquiry. As we venture further into the digital era, the interplay between technology, media, and folklore will undoubtedly continue to shape and redefine the Yeti's place in popular culture and scientific discourse.

The Yeti in Contemporary Reporting and Exploration

The Yeti, often known as the Abominable Snowman, has been a subject of intrigue and mystery, captivating the imagination of explorers, scientists, and the general public alike. Contemporary reporting and exploration have played a pivotal role in both perpetuating and demystifying the legend of the Yeti.

Scientific Exploration and Genetic Analysis

Recent scientific studies have focused on analyzing physical specimens attributed to the Yeti, such as hair, bone, and skin. Two significant studies published in the Proceedings of the Royal Society B have brought new insights into this enigma. A 2014 study concluded that the genetic evidence from these specimens mostly came from a range of known animals. Another study in 2017 found that all but one of these samples came from bears, with the outlier being from a dog. These findings suggest that the biological basis of the Yeti legend is likely local brown and black bears.

Cultural Interpretations and Misunderstandings

The Yeti's existence, while not supported by conclusive scientific evidence, continues to be a part of the folklore and spiritual beliefs in the Himalayas. This creature is deeply ingrained in the pre-Buddhist mythology of several Himalayan peoples and later integrated into Buddhist mythology. For instance, there are tales of Yetis helping important religious figures, such as the story of a Yeti assisting the Buddhist Master Lama Sange Dorje around 600 years ago. The Yeti is often viewed as a rare, flesh-and-bones creature with supernatural powers, a perspective that contrasts with the Western view of it as a cryptozoological hoax.

Contemporary Sightings and Reports

Despite the scientific debunking, reports and sightings of the Yeti continue in the Himalayas. These accounts often describe encounters with large, hairy, ape-like creatures, fueling ongoing interest and speculation. For many locals in the Himalayan region, Tibet, and parts of highland Central Asia, the Yeti remains a real entity, necessitating protection like any other rare species. For example, in Bhutan, a national park has been established specifically to provide a safe area for Yetis, believed to be abundant in the region.

The Yeti in Modern Context

The Yeti's place in contemporary culture and exploration is a complex blend of science, folklore, and public fascination. While scientific research leans towards a rational explanation linking Yeti legends to bears, the myth continues to thrive in local cultures and among enthusiasts worldwide. The legend of the Yeti, thus, remains a compelling narrative, straddling the line between myth and reality, and continues to inspire explorers and researchers in their quest to understand the mysteries of the natural world.

Technology and Future Discoveries in Yeti Research

The quest for the Yeti, an enigmatic figure in folklore and cryptozoology, has been significantly influenced by technological advancements. This chapter explores the role of contemporary technology in Yeti research and the potential for future discoveries.

Advancements in Technology Enhancing Yeti Research

The technological revolution has had a profound impact on Yeti research. Modern tools and methods have offered new ways to explore remote Himalayan regions, thought to be the home of the Yeti. Technologies such as satellite imaging, drones, and advanced camera traps are now pivotal in surveying these inaccessible areas. These tools not only enable researchers to cover vast expanses of terrain but also minimize the risks and challenges of physical expeditions.

Genetic Analysis: A Pathway to Unraveling Mysteries

Genetic analysis has become a cornerstone in the search for the Yeti. Studies analyzing DNA from purported Yeti samples have brought significant insights. A notable example is the work published in the Proceedings of the Royal Society B, which concluded that most samples attributed to the Yeti were from known animals like bears. These genetic studies, while often debunking the existence of a novel species, have also opened avenues for understanding the biodiversity of the Himalayan region, including rare and endangered species.

The Role of Environmental DNA (eDNA) in Cryptozoology

Environmental DNA (eDNA) analysis is a burgeoning field that holds promise in Yeti research. This technique involves collecting and examining genetic material from environmental samples like soil, water, or snow. eDNA could potentially detect the presence of elusive or unknown species without the need for physical specimens. If the Yeti or a similar unknown creature exists, eDNA could provide credible evidence of its presence.

Technology in Myth-Busting and Education

Technology has also played a critical role in debunking myths and educating the public about the Yeti. Documentaries, virtual reality experiences, and interactive digital platforms have been instrumental in disseminating factual information. These mediums not only explore the legend of the Yeti but also delve into the science behind the research, helping demystify the topic for a broader audience.

Future Technologies and Exploration

Looking forward, advancements in technology will continue to shape Yeti research. Developments in artificial intelligence, machine learning, and robotics could revolutionize data analysis and field exploration. For instance, AI-driven analysis of vast datasets could identify patterns or anomalies that human researchers might miss. Similarly, robots or autonomous vehicles could be deployed in harsh or dangerous terrains, opening new frontiers in the exploration of remote Himalayan regions.

In the realm of Yeti research, technology serves as both a tool for exploration and a means for scientific verification. While technological advancements have largely challenged the existence of the Yeti as a distinct species, they have simultaneously enhanced our understanding of the rich biodiversity and ecological complexity of the Himalayas. As technology continues to evolve, it will undoubtedly provide new perspectives and insights into the enduring mystery of the Yeti.

The Role of Technology in Yeti Research

The pursuit of the Yeti, a creature shrouded in myth and mystery, has entered a new phase with the advent of modern technology. This chapter explores how technological advancements are reshaping Yeti research, offering new insights and challenging long-standing beliefs.

DNA Analysis: Unraveling the Yeti Mystery

One of the most significant technological advancements in Yeti research is DNA analysis. In recent studies, DNA testing of various samples thought to be from the Yeti revealed that they were, in fact, from known animal species. A comprehensive study involving nine samples from the Himalayas and the Tibetan Plateau, including hair, skin, tooth, bone, and fecal matter, showed that all but one were from bears – specifically, Asian black bears, Himalayan brown bears, or Tibetan brown bears. The exception was a tooth that turned out to be from a domestic dog. This groundbreaking research suggests that the biological basis of the Yeti legend likely stems from local bear populations. Charlotte Lindqvist, a biologist from the University at Buffalo College of Arts and Sciences, emphasizes that genetics can unravel other similar mysteries, demonstrating that the legend may have evolved from encounters with real animals.

Theoretical Speculations and Academic Perspectives

Theories about the Yeti's existence have varied, ranging from surviving collateral hominid species like Homo neanderthalensis or Homo floresiensis to large primates like Gigantopithecus, thought to be extinct. Mainstream science, however, remains skeptical due to the lack of testable evidence and the possibility of fraudulent claims. The introduction of sophisticated genetic analysis techniques offers a method for genus and species identification that is unbiased and impervious to falsification. This approach was not available to early biologists like Dr. Bernard Heuvelmans, whose work fostered widespread public interest in cryptids. Today, researchers like Professor Bryan Sykes and Michel Sartori are examining these neglected specimens to gain deeper insights into the interaction and spread of Neanderthals and other early hominids.

Future Directions in Yeti Research

As technology continues to advance, it opens up new possibilities for Yeti research. Genetic analysis has already changed the narrative by providing scientific explanations for previously unexplained phenomena. Future technological advancements, such as more sophisticated DNA sequencing and environmental DNA (eDNA) analysis, could further illuminate the mysteries surrounding the Yeti. These methods could potentially identify genetic material in environmental samples like soil or snow, offering a non-invasive way to explore the existence of elusive species.

The integration of technology into Yeti research represents a significant shift from myth and folklore to scientific inquiry. While technology has challenged the existence of the Yeti as a distinct species, it has also deepened our understanding of the biodiversity in the Himalayan region. The role of technology in Yeti research is not just about proving or disproving the existence of a mythical creature; it's about expanding our knowledge of the natural world and the creatures that inhabit it. As we move forward, technology will undoubtedly continue to play a pivotal role in unraveling the mysteries of the Yeti.

Technological Advancements in Cryptozoology: Tools and Techniques

The field of cryptozoology, particularly in the research of cryptids like the Yeti, has been profoundly impacted by technological advancements. This chapter delves into the tools and techniques that are reshaping the way researchers approach the study of elusive creatures.

Modern Genetic Analysis

DNA analysis has revolutionized the study of cryptids, providing an empirical basis for investigations. The use of DNA testing on samples thought to be from the Yeti has yielded enlightening results. For instance, a study analyzing various samples like hair, bone, and skin found that most were from known animals such as bears. This research, involving advanced techniques like PCR amplification, mitochondrial sequencing, and phylogenetic analysis, demonstrates how genetic tools can help differentiate between myth and reality in cryptozoology.

Advances in Field Research Technology

The exploration of remote areas where cryptids are said to reside has been greatly enhanced by technology. Drones, camera traps, and satellite imaging enable researchers to survey inaccessible regions with minimal risk. These tools allow for the collection of data from environments where cryptids like the Yeti are rumored to exist, providing invaluable information about these elusive creatures' possible habitats.

Environmental DNA (eDNA)

Environmental DNA analysis is an emerging tool in cryptozoology. It involves extracting genetic material from environmental samples such as soil, water, or snow. This technique can potentially detect traces of elusive species, including cryptids, without the need for physical specimens. eDNA analysis offers a non-invasive approach to cryptozoological research, opening new possibilities for detecting and studying cryptids in their natural habitats.

Cryptid Research Archives and Databases

Technological advancements have also facilitated the creation and maintenance of extensive archives and databases. These resources compile historical accounts, eyewitness reports, and physical evidence related to cryptids. For instance, the Museum of Zoology in Lausanne, Switzerland, curates an archive assembled by Dr. Bernard Heuvelmans, a pioneer in cryptozoology. Such archives are invaluable for researchers looking to cross-reference and analyze data from various sources and time periods.

The Integration of AI and Machine Learning

Artificial intelligence (AI) and machine learning are emerging as powerful tools in cryptozoology. AI can process and analyze large datasets, identifying patterns or anomalies that may indicate the presence of a cryptid. Machine learning algorithms can be trained to recognize and categorize evidence, enhancing the efficiency and accuracy of cryptozoological research.

Future Prospects and Challenges

Looking ahead, technology is likely to continue to play a crucial role in cryptozoology. The development of more sophisticated DNA sequencing techniques, enhanced AI algorithms, and innovative field equipment will likely provide deeper insights into the existence and nature of cryptids like the Yeti. However, the challenge remains in balancing technological advancement with ethical considerations, such as respecting local cultures and preserving the natural habitats of potential cryptids.

Technological advancements in cryptozoology are transforming the field, providing new tools and techniques to investigate the existence of cryptids. From genetic analysis to AI and machine learning, these developments offer promising pathways to uncover the truths behind longstanding myths and legends. As technology evolves, it will undoubtedly continue to shape the future of cryptozoological research.

Chapter 9
Philosophical Perspectives: Myth and Reality

The pursuit of the Yeti, entrenched in the realms of cryptozoology and folklore, presents an intriguing case for philosophical examination. This chapter delves into the philosophical aspects surrounding the Yeti, exploring the interplay between myth and reality, belief and skepticism, and the nature of scientific inquiry.

Myth and Reality: The Yeti as a Philosophical Enigma

The Yeti, often considered a cryptid or mythical creature, raises important philosophical questions about the distinction between myth and reality. Myths, across various cultures, are not merely fanciful stories but serve as mediums to convey deeper truths or understandings about the world. The Yeti, deeply rooted in the folklore of the Himalayas, symbolizes more than a mysterious creature; it represents the unknown, the unexplored, and the possibility of undiscovered entities in nature. The philosophical debate hinges on whether the Yeti should be regarded purely as a mythical entity or as a subject warranting scientific inquiry.

The Nature of Belief and Skepticism

The belief in the Yeti's existence, despite scant empirical evidence, brings to light the complex nature of belief systems. It raises questions about what constitutes sufficient evidence for belief and how folklore and anecdotal experiences influence our perception of reality. The skepticism surrounding the Yeti's existence, on the other hand, underscores the importance of empirical evidence and scientific validation in establishing the truth. This dichotomy between belief and skepticism is central to the philosophical discourse on the Yeti.

Scientific Inquiry and the Limits of Knowledge

The Yeti's elusive nature also presents a philosophical inquiry into the nature and limits of scientific knowledge. It prompts the question: what are the boundaries of scientific understanding, and how does science contend with phenomena that are yet unproven but not entirely disprovable? The pursuit of the Yeti in scientific terms – through genetic analysis and field research – reflects an endeavor to extend these boundaries, exploring the unknown and expanding our comprehension of the natural world.

Ethical Considerations in Cryptozoological Research

Philosophically, Yeti research also raises ethical questions. It prompts a reflection on the impact of such research on indigenous cultures for whom the Yeti holds significant cultural and spiritual value. Moreover, it invites discussion on the ethics of exploration and the potential risks to ecosystems and species in pursuit of cryptids. Balancing scientific curiosity with respect for nature and cultural heritage is a crucial aspect of the philosophical discourse surrounding the Yeti.

The Yeti, straddling the line between myth and reality, serves as a profound subject for philosophical exploration. It challenges us to consider the nature of belief, the extent of scientific knowledge, and the ethical dimensions of exploring the unknown. The philosophical perspectives on the Yeti not only enrich our understanding of this enigmatic creature but also offer deeper insights into human curiosity, the pursuit of knowledge, and the complexities of interpreting the world around us.

The Yeti and the Nature of Reality: Philosophical Implications

The Yeti, a creature steeped in myth and legend, particularly in the Himalayan region, presents a fascinating intersection of folklore, scientific inquiry, and philosophical discourse on the nature of reality. Its existence, while not scientifically substantiated, continues to captivate the imagination and challenge our understanding of what is real and what is mythical.

In the realm of folklore, the Yeti holds a significant place among the indigenous people of the Himalayas, like the Lepcha, who view it as an ape-like glacier spirit influential in the success of hunting trips. This intersection of the real and unreal, where mythical powers intermingle with supposed physical sightings, blurs the lines between mythology and physical existence.

Scientific expeditions have sought to uncover the truth behind the Yeti legend, proposing various theories like the Yeti being a rare bear species or a surviving hominid. These scientific inquiries, however, often clash with the lack of concrete evidence, leading to skepticism among the scientific community.

Philosophically, the discourse on the nature of reality provides a broader context in which to understand the Yeti phenomenon. Reality, as conceptualized in various philosophical traditions, is independent of our perception or understanding of it. For instance, Immanuel Kant posited that we can never truly know reality in itself (the noumenal world), as our perceptions are always subject to the limitations and constructs of our minds (the phenomenal world).

From the perspective of idealists, reality fundamentally consists of consciousness and mental constructs. Everything, including physical entities like particles and brains, is conceptualized as ideas within consciousness. This stance raises intriguing questions about the Yeti's existence, suggesting that whether the Yeti is 'real' may depend more on our perceptions and collective consciousness than on empirical evidence.

The debate on metaphysical realism, the view that entities exist independently of our knowledge or perception of them, further complicates our understanding of entities like the Yeti. Some philosophers argue for a mind-independent existence of entities, while others, like Rudolf Carnap, view statements asserting the reality of entities as devoid of cognitive content, focusing instead on practical language use to describe observable phenomena.

In this philosophical landscape, the Yeti's existence is not merely a question of empirical evidence but also of how we construct and perceive reality. It challenges the boundaries between the physical and the metaphysical, the empirical and the mythical, urging us to consider the deeper implications of what we deem real and unreal. The Yeti, therefore, becomes a symbol of the human quest to understand the nature of reality, blending scientific curiosity, cultural mythology, and philosophical inquiry.

Ethical Considerations: Research and Discovery

The exploration and study of cryptids like the Yeti, often categorized under cryptozoology, present unique ethical considerations. Cryptozoology, the search for and study of creatures whose existence is not yet proven, such as the Yeti, intersects various disciplines and calls into question the ethical dimensions of research and discovery in this field.

The Ethical Dilemma in Cryptozoological Research

The pursuit of cryptozoology often leads to speculative conclusions, heavily relying on eyewitness accounts and folklore. For instance, speculative zoology, a part of cryptozoology, involves imaginative assumptions about the existence and characteristics of these cryptids. Belgian zoologist Bernard Heuvelmans, a prominent figure in cryptozoology, categorized sea monsters and Eurasian ape-men (Yeti) using eyewitness sightings, leading to speculative theories far removed from empirical evidence. This speculative nature raises questions about the scientific integrity of such studies and the ethical responsibility of researchers to adhere to rigorous scientific methods.

This ethical challenge is further complicated by the fact that cryptozoology is not a subset of biological science but rather a psychological and sociocultural phenomenon. The perception of cryptids like the Yeti is significantly influenced by cultural narratives and personal expectations. Consequently, the field has been viewed skeptically, often considered as fringe or pseudoscience, with a tendency to attract a range of beliefs including creationism and conspiracy theories. This has led to debates over the legitimacy and scientific value of cryptozoological research.

Responsible Research Practices

Despite these challenges, not all cryptozoologists disregard scientific principles. There exists within the community a commitment to data collection and respect for the scientific process. Honest skepticism and a scientific approach are present among researchers who seek to understand these cryptids within the realm of possibility, guided by empirical evidence rather than mere speculation or folklore. This adherence to scientific integrity is crucial in maintaining ethical standards in cryptozoological research.

The complexity of cryptozoology as a field lies in its interplay between myth, folklore, and the desire for empirical validation. Researchers in this field must navigate the thin line between respecting cultural narratives and maintaining scientific rigor. The ethical responsibility, therefore, extends beyond mere adherence to scientific methodology; it includes the consideration of cultural sensitivities, the potential impact of research findings on local communities, and the implications of presenting speculative theories as scientific facts.

The study of the Yeti and other cryptids demands a careful ethical balance. Researchers must critically evaluate the validity of their methods and findings, considering the broader implications of their work. This includes acknowledging the psychological and sociocultural aspects of cryptozoology, ensuring scientific integrity, and respecting the cultural contexts from which these legends emerge. Ethical research in cryptozoology should aim to contribute to our understanding of the natural world, while also respecting the myths and folklore that give these cryptids their enduring allure.

Beyond the Yeti: Philosophical Insights

The pursuit of creatures like the Yeti, nestled within the field of cryptozoology, not only challenges the frontiers of scientific knowledge but also invites profound philosophical considerations. This journey into the unknown is marked by an interplay of perception, culture, and the relentless human quest for understanding the mysterious.

The Intersection of Perception and Belief

Perception plays a pivotal role in shaping beliefs within cryptozoology. It's a field where the interpretation of evidence is heavily influenced by cultural and societal norms. For instance, in some indigenous North American cultures, belief in creatures like the Yeti is an accepted fact, deeply rooted in cultural heritage. In contrast, many contemporary societies view such beliefs as mere folklore or superstition. However, the rise of social media and the internet has paradoxically led to an increase in belief and interest in these creatures.

Religion, too, shapes perceptions in cryptozoology. Across different cultures, religious and mythological narratives often include cryptids, thereby influencing how these creatures are perceived and understood. For instance, creatures akin to the Yeti in Hindu mythology are seen as divine, while in western Catholicism, they are often viewed as demonic.

The Role of Scientific Inquiry and Discoveries

The search for cryptids like the Yeti has occasionally led to significant scientific discoveries, even if the cryptids themselves remain elusive. This is exemplified by the discovery of new animal species that were once considered mythical, such as the gorilla, the platypus, and the Komodo dragon. These discoveries underscore that mysterious animals don't exclusively reveal themselves to scientists but can be observed by anyone, regardless of their professional background.

The collaboration between cryptozoologists and mainstream scientists has occasionally yielded unexpected results. For example, in the search for the Yeti, scientists were able to sequence the mitochondrial genomes of Himalayan brown bear and black bear for the first time, providing valuable insights into their evolutionary history.

The Philosophical Dimension

At its core, the exploration of cryptids like the Yeti transcends the boundaries of empirical science and delves into philosophical territories. It raises fundamental questions about the nature of knowledge, the limits of scientific understanding, and the human inclination towards exploring the unknown. The pursuit of these elusive creatures is a testament to the human spirit's insatiable curiosity and its unyielding desire to make sense of the world, even when faced with the inexplicable.

In essence, the search for the Yeti and similar cryptids is a reflection of humanity's eternal quest for knowledge and understanding. It challenges us to constantly reevaluate our perceptions, beliefs, and the very nature of reality as we know it. This journey, although fraught with uncertainties and skepticism, continues to captivate and inspire, reminding us of the endless possibilities that lie in the unexplored corners of our world and our understanding.

The Yeti in Literature and Art: Cultural Reflections

The Yeti, or Abominable Snowman, has captured human imagination not only through folklore and eyewitness accounts but also through its vivid portrayal in literature and art. This mythical creature has been represented in various forms, ranging from fearsome to friendly, reflecting diverse cultural perceptions and artistic interpretations.

The Yeti in Literature

In literature, the Yeti has been featured in numerous works, often embodying the mysterious and unknown aspects of nature. For instance, Hergé's comic book "Tintin in Tibet" (1958-1959) presents the Yeti as an enormous, intelligent, and sensitive creature, a significant departure from its usual portrayal as a mere beast. This representation reflects a deeper understanding and compassion for the mythical creature, illustrating its potential for benevolence.

Harry Turtledove, in his "State of Jefferson Stories," explores the Yeti, Sasquatches, and other cryptids in a unique light. Unlike common depictions of these creatures as less evolved primates, Turtledove portrays them as another race of human beings, integrated into society. This approach in literature challenges the conventional portrayal of cryptids and invites readers to consider them from a more humane and inclusive perspective.

The Yeti in Film and Animation

In the realm of film and animation, the Yeti has been a popular character, often depicted in a manner that appeals to a broad audience. Animated films like "Smallfoot" (2018) and "Abominable" (2019) have portrayed Yetis in imaginative ways, with "Smallfoot" depicting them as 20-foot-tall creatures with horns on their heads and "Abominable" featuring a young Yeti named Everest as a central character.

These films, through their creative renditions, contribute to the cultural and artistic landscape of the Yeti mythology, offering new dimensions to its character and story. They also reflect the shifting perceptions of the Yeti in popular culture, from a creature of folklore to a character of mainstream entertainment.

The Yeti in Popular Culture

The Yeti's presence in popular culture is marked by a variety of portrayals, often influenced by the artistic choices based on its snowy habitat. For instance, the trademark white fur of the Yeti in many artistic renditions is more of an artistic choice rather than a reflection of eyewitness reports, which often describe it with reddish-brown fur. This artistic liberty highlights the role of cultural and environmental context in shaping the depiction of mythical creatures like the Yeti.

The representation of the Yeti in literature and art is a testament to the enduring fascination and curiosity that this mythical creature inspires. From comics and novels to films and animations, the Yeti continues to be a source of creative inspiration, reflecting the diverse ways in which humans interact with and interpret the mysteries of the natural world. The Yeti's portrayal across various media not only entertains but also invites reflection on the broader themes of mystery, nature, and the unknown.

The Yeti in Artistic Expression: Visual and Literary Forms

The Yeti, a figure shrouded in myth and mystery, has not only captivated the realm of folklore but has also significantly influenced artistic expression, both visually and in literature. The enigmatic nature of the Yeti has sparked the imagination of artists and writers, leading to a rich tapestry of portrayals that span a broad spectrum of styles and interpretations.

Artistic Interpretations in Visual Arts

In visual arts, the Yeti has been a subject of fascination and inspiration. Artists have often used the Yeti as a symbol to explore themes of mystery, wilderness, and the unknown. The depiction of the Yeti varies greatly, with some artists choosing to represent it in a form consistent with traditional eyewitness reports, portraying it as a large, bipedal creature covered in reddish-brown fur. Others, however, have adopted more imaginative and stylized representations, often influenced by the Yeti's snowy habitat, leading to the depiction of the creature with white fur, which is a deviation from the traditional descriptions reported in sightings.

Artists at Yeti Designs, for example, embark on a creative process that blends conscious planning with spontaneous expression. Their works often represent a dance between the conscious and subconscious, where each stroke and sculpting decision contributes to the final piece, embodying the mystery and allure of the Yeti. This artistic journey is one of constant refinement, exploring new techniques and pushing boundaries, thus adding depth and diversity to the portrayal of the Yeti in visual arts.

Literary Expressions and Comic Representations

In literature, the Yeti has been featured in various narratives, ranging from stories that depict it as a gentle giant to those that portray it as a fearsome beast. The Yeti's literary presence offers a window into different cultural interpretations and understandings of this elusive creature.

The Yeti's influence extends to the world of comics, where it has been featured in diverse roles and settings. For example, the exhibition "Hero, Villain, Yeti: Tibet in Comics" showcased a collection of comic books from around the world, reflecting on the depiction of Tibet and the Yeti. These comics spanned various genres, including fantasy, biography, politics, and education, illustrating the Yeti's versatile role in storytelling.

The Yeti's Influence Across Cultures

The Yeti's representation in both visual and literary forms highlights its impact on global culture. While the creature's origins lie in the folklore of the Himalayas, its artistic and literary depictions have transcended geographical boundaries, resonating with audiences worldwide. This wide-ranging influence is a testament to the Yeti's enduring appeal and its ability to inspire creativity across different mediums and cultures.

The Yeti's presence in artistic expression, be it in visual arts or literature, is a reflection of humanity's fascination with the mysterious and the unknown. Through various artistic mediums, the Yeti continues to captivate the imagination, challenging our perceptions and inviting us to explore the deeper meanings behind this enigmatic figure.

The Yeti in Science Fiction and Fantasy: Imaginative Interpretations

The Yeti, also known as the Abominable Snowman, has not only been a subject of intrigue in folklore and cryptozoology but has also found a prominent place in the realms of science fiction and fantasy. This legendary creature, often depicted as a large, ape-like being dwelling in the Himalayan mountains, has inspired various imaginative interpretations in literature, reflecting the human fascination with the unknown and the mysterious.

The Yeti in Science Fiction

In science fiction, the Yeti often appears as a creature from another world or dimension, sometimes portrayed with advanced intelligence or unique abilities. This genre allows for a reimagining of the Yeti beyond the traditional myths, often placing it in futuristic or alternative reality settings. For example, the category of "Yeti in fiction" on Wikipedia lists various instances where the Yeti has been featured in science fiction narratives, ranging from TV series to novels, showcasing the creature's adaptability to diverse sci-fi contexts.

One notable example of the Yeti in science fiction is in the various adaptations of "Doctor Who," where the Yeti is depicted as a robot used by an extraterrestrial entity known as the Great Intelligence.

These interpretations provide a unique twist to the traditional Yeti myth, blending elements of technology and alien involvement.

The Yeti in Fantasy Literature

In fantasy literature, the Yeti is often portrayed in a more mystical and magical context. It is not uncommon to find the Yeti depicted as a wise, elusive creature, sometimes with magical powers, in these stories. The fantasy genre provides a rich landscape for exploring the Yeti's mythical and mysterious nature, often integrating it into elaborate world-building and complex narratives.

For instance, in "Tintin in Tibet," a classic comic by Hergé, the Yeti is depicted as an empathetic creature showing kindness and intelligence. This portrayal challenges the often fearsome image of the Yeti, presenting it as capable of complex emotions and actions.

The Yeti in Science Fiction Romances

A fascinating and perhaps unexpected development in Yeti-themed literature is its appearance in science fiction romances. This sub-genre often portrays the Yeti in romantic narratives, sometimes even as a love interest. For example, "Snowed in with the Yeti: An Erotic Monster Romance" by Brigid Finn is set in a post-apocalyptic world and features a Yeti character in a romantic context. Such narratives explore the Yeti myth from a completely different perspective, focusing on emotional connections and relationships.

The Yeti's presence in science fiction and fantasy literature is a testament to its enduring allure and the human penchant for exploring the unknown through storytelling. Whether portrayed as a mysterious creature of the mountains, a robotic entity from another world, or a character in a romantic tale, the Yeti continues to captivate the imagination of writers and readers alike, proving that its myth transcends cultural and genre boundaries.

The Yeti in Adventure and Exploration: The Lure of the Unknown

The Yeti, a creature of legend and folklore, has long been a source of fascination and mystery, inspiring numerous adventures and explorations in the rugged terrains of the Himalayas. These quests, driven by the allure of the unknown and the desire to unveil the truth behind the myth, have shaped our understanding of the Yeti and its place in the world of exploration.

The Himalayan Yeti: Mythology and Folklore

The Himalayan Yeti, deeply rooted in the mythology of the Himalayan region, is often depicted as a supernatural being with incredible strength and abilities. Regarded as a protector of the mountains, the Yeti is revered by local communities like the Sherpas and Tibetans, each having their unique versions of the mythical creature. These cultural narratives paint the Yeti as an integral part of their identity and beliefs, adding layers of mystique to the legend.

Expeditions in Search of the Yeti

Numerous expeditions have ventured into the Himalayas in pursuit of the Yeti, often returning with more questions than answers. One of the most famous expeditions was led by Sir Edmund Hillary in 1960, which focused on investigating the existence of the Yeti. The expedition's findings, including a peculiar skull, later revealed to be that of a rare Tibetan antelope, added to the scientific skepticism regarding the Yeti's existence.

Another notable expedition was the Silver Hut expedition, which included a comprehensive search for the Yeti. Despite their efforts, using advanced technology for the time, the expedition did not yield any conclusive evidence of the Yeti's existence. The efforts included setting up traps and using tranquilizer-loaded guns, telescopes, and microphones to capture any signs of the elusive creature.

The Role of Skepticism and Hoaxes

While some expeditions have claimed sightings and encounters with the Yeti, many of these have been met with skepticism. The lack of concrete evidence and the prevalence of hoaxes and misidentifications have cast doubt on the authenticity of many alleged Yeti sightings. For example, some reported Yeti encounters were later revealed to be men dressed in fur suits or misidentified animals.

The Impact of Yeti Expeditions on Conservation

As the legend of the Yeti continues to captivate the imagination of explorers and adventurers, it raises questions about the creature's conservation and preservation. While concrete evidence of the Yeti's existence remains elusive, the discussions and debates spurred by these explorations have brought attention to the need for preserving the natural habitats of the Himalayas, which are under threat from climate change and human development.

The quest for the Yeti represents a fascinating chapter in the history of adventure and exploration. It is a journey fueled by the human desire to explore the unknown, to challenge our understanding of the natural world, and to confront the mysteries that lie in the uncharted territories of our planet. The Yeti, whether myth or reality, continues to inspire adventurers and researchers alike, embodying the enduring allure of the unexplained and the undiscovered.

The Yeti in the World of Cryptozoology: A Critical View

In the diverse and often controversial world of cryptozoology, the Yeti stands as one of the most iconic and enigmatic subjects. Cryptozoology, the study of creatures whose existence is unsubstantiated by mainstream science, has long been fascinated by the legend of the Yeti, a creature purported to inhabit the Himalayan region. This chapter delves into the critical perspectives within cryptozoology regarding the Yeti, exploring the intersection of science, myth, and the ongoing quest for understanding unexplained phenomena.

The Scientific Skepticism Surrounding the Yeti

The quest for the Yeti in cryptozoology often clashes with the rigorous demands of scientific evidence. Despite numerous expeditions and investigations, conclusive evidence of the Yeti's existence remains elusive. Scientists and skeptics argue that most Yeti sightings can be attributed to misidentified wildlife, such as bears or langurs, or are outright hoaxes. The scientific community demands empirical evidence, such as DNA samples, that unequivocally prove the Yeti's existence, which has not been forthcoming.

Debunking Myths and Misidentifications

Many supposed Yeti sightings and evidences have been debunked over the years. For instance, the famous 1951 photograph of a Yeti footprint by Eric Shipton has been subject to much scrutiny. Some experts suggest that the print could have been made by a bear, distorted by the melting snow. Similarly, alleged Yeti hair samples analyzed in various studies often turned out to be from known animals like bears or bovids.

The Role of Culture and Folklore in Perpetuating the Yeti Legend

The Yeti is deeply ingrained in the folklore and culture of the Himalayan region. Local communities have various names and attributes for the creature, often regarded as a spiritual entity or guardian of the mountains. This cultural aspect plays a significant role in keeping the legend alive, influencing the perception and interpretation of potential evidence. However, the intertwining of cultural beliefs and scientific inquiry complicates the objective study of the Yeti in cryptozoology.

The Impact of Cryptozoology on Conservation Efforts

Cryptozoology, despite its controversial standing in the scientific community, has indirectly contributed to conservation efforts. The interest in cryptids like the Yeti often brings attention to the ecological and environmental issues in their supposed habitats. For instance, the Himalayan region, home to the Yeti legend, is a biodiversity hotspot facing threats from climate change and human activities. The fascination with the Yeti can help highlight the need for conservation in these sensitive ecological areas.

The Yeti's place in cryptozoology is a testament to the enduring human fascination with the unknown and unexplained. While the scientific community remains skeptical, the quest for the Yeti continues to inspire adventurers, researchers, and enthusiasts. This pursuit, albeit fraught with challenges and controversies, underscores the complex relationship between myth, culture, and science in our understanding of the natural world. The Yeti, whether real or mythical, serves as a symbol of the mysteries that still captivate our imagination and the uncharted frontiers of our knowledge.

The Yeti and Human Imagination: Exploring the Myth

The Yeti, an enigmatic creature shrouded in mystery, has long captivated human imagination, spawning a rich tapestry of myths, legends, and speculative theories. This chapter explores the intricate relationship between the Yeti myth and the human psyche, delving into how this legendary creature continues to stimulate curiosity, fear, and wonder.

The Yeti: A Symbol of the Unexplored

The Yeti symbolizes the unexplored and unknown aspects of our world. In many cultures, particularly in the Himalayas, it represents the mysteries that lie in the remote and inaccessible corners of the Earth. The allure of the Yeti lies in its ability to embody the human quest for exploration and the desire to understand the mysteries of nature. The fact that the Yeti has remained elusive despite numerous expeditions and technological advancements further adds to its mystique.

Cultural Impact of the Yeti Myth

The Yeti's presence in folklore and popular culture is significant. It has been depicted in various forms, from a fearsome beast to a guardian of the mountains. This varied portrayal reflects the cultural and psychological nuances associated with the Yeti. In Himalayan communities, the Yeti is often intertwined with spiritual beliefs and is considered a part of their cultural heritage.

The Yeti in Modern Media and Entertainment

In modern times, the Yeti has found its way into films, literature, and even video games, often depicted as a character that oscillates between being a formidable antagonist and a misunderstood creature. The portrayal of the Yeti in media often mirrors contemporary societal themes, such as the fear of the unknown or the clash between civilization and nature.

Psychological Perspectives on the Yeti Phenomenon

From a psychological standpoint, the Yeti can be seen as a manifestation of the human tendency to personify fear and curiosity. The unknown nature of the Yeti allows people to project their fears, hopes, and imaginations onto it. This phenomenon is not just limited to the Yeti but is a common aspect of human psychology where unknown entities become canvases for our deepest emotions and thoughts.

The Role of the Yeti in Science and Skepticism

The Yeti also plays a pivotal role in the dialogue between science and skepticism. While science demands empirical evidence for the Yeti's existence, the lack of conclusive proof does not deter the fascination and belief in the creature. This interplay highlights the complex relationship between belief, folklore, and scientific inquiry, showcasing how myths and legends can endure even in the face of scientific skepticism.

The Yeti, as a cultural and psychological symbol, continues to be a source of fascination and intrigue. It represents the human spirit's relentless pursuit of understanding the unknown. The Yeti's enduring presence in human imagination serves as a reminder of the mysteries that still exist in our world and our unceasing desire to explore them. Whether real or mythical, the Yeti remains an integral part of our collective imagination, embodying the mystery, fear, and wonder that define the human experience.

Chapter 10
Yeti Encounter 3 - The Russian Enigma

The Siberian Discovery

In the vast and often unforgiving wilderness of Siberia, a story of intrigue and mystery unfolds, one that challenges the boundaries of known science and delves into the realm of legend. This account, as narrated by Dr. Alexei Ivanov, a respected Russian zoologist, begins in the spring of 1992 when a team of scientists embarked on an expedition to explore the remote and rarely traversed regions of the Siberian taiga.

Dr. Ivanov, a man of science with a healthy skepticism for the unproven, had spent years studying the wildlife of Siberia. His interest in the Yeti, or 'Khomani' as known in local lore, was purely academic, driven more by the need to debunk myths than to confirm them. However, this expedition, funded by the Russian Academy of

Sciences, aimed to investigate recent reports of unusual animal activity in the Kemerovo region, a place long shrouded in mystery and folklore.

The team, consisting of biologists, anthropologists, and a seasoned local guide, embarked from Novosibirsk, journeying deep into the heart of the taiga. The landscape was a mosaic of dense forests and rugged mountains, where nature reigned supreme, untouched by the hand of man. Dr. Ivanov described the first days of the expedition as routine, filled with the cataloging of flora and fauna, and the collection of soil and water samples.

But it was on the fourth day that the ordinary course of their research took an unexpected turn. As they navigated a particularly dense part of the forest, they stumbled upon a series of large, unusual footprints. Dr. Ivanov, initially dismissive, took a closer interest when he realized that the prints did not match any known wildlife in the region. The footprints were oddly human-like but much larger, with a strange gait pattern that suggested a creature of considerable size.

The discovery prompted a change in the expedition's focus. Driven by a mix of scientific curiosity and a hint of the unexplained, they decided to follow the trail. The footprints led them through the forest and up a steep ridge, where the treacherous terrain made progress painstakingly slow.

As night fell, they set up camp in a small clearing, the air filled with the sounds of the Siberian wilderness. That night, Dr. Ivanov recalled hearing a series of distant, unidentifiable sounds that seemed neither animal nor human. The team, though seasoned in the field, felt an unspoken unease, a sense that they were not alone in the vast expanse of the forest.

The following morning revealed an even more baffling discovery – a small, makeshift structure nestled against a rocky outcrop, seemingly constructed from branches and foliage. Inside, they found what appeared to be a rudimentary bed made of leaves and animal furs. Samples were collected for analysis, but Dr. Ivanov remained cautious, wary of jumping to conclusions.

The team's journey continued, tracing the mysterious footprints that seemed to lead them deeper into the heart of the Siberian taiga. Each step took them further from the known and closer to the shadowy realm of legend. Dr. Ivanov, a man of logic and reason, found himself questioning the nature of their discovery, torn between the rational world of science and the tantalizing possibility of the unknown.

The Veil of Mystery Deepens

The Siberian expedition led by Dr. Alexei Ivanov, now deep within the uncharted territories of the Kemerovo region, found themselves on a path that was increasingly diverging from the realm of known science. With each step, the mysteries they encountered compounded, pulling them into a narrative that seemed to belong more to folklore than to the annals of zoology.

As they followed the trail of the enigmatic footprints, the forest around them grew denser, the trees like silent sentinels guarding ancient secrets. The air was thick with the scent of pine and the damp earth, a stark reminder of the wilderness that enveloped them.

One morning, amidst the chorus of birds and the rustling of leaves, the team stumbled upon a new clue – a series of coarse, dark hairs snagged on the bark of a pine tree. Dr. Ivanov, with his keen scientific acumen, carefully collected the samples, though he remained skeptical, suspecting they could belong to one of the region's large mammals, perhaps a bear.

However, it was later that day when the expedition's narrative took a dramatic turn. While navigating a particularly rugged ridge, they came across an abandoned cabin, its wooden frame weathered by time and elements. The cabin, seemingly untouched for years, contained remnants of human habitation – a rusted kettle, a broken chair, and tattered remnants of clothing.

As they examined the cabin, Dr. Ivanov's attention was drawn to a series of faded photographs pinned to the wall. They depicted scenes of the surrounding wilderness, and in one, a figure stood in the distance, partially obscured by the trees. The figure was indistinct, yet its form suggested something other than human, something that resonated with the tales of the Khomani.

The discovery sent a ripple of excitement through the team, a mixture of apprehension and exhilaration. The cabin, with its mysterious occupant and its connection to the footprints and hairs they had found, seemed to be a piece of a puzzle that was slowly coming together.

That evening, as they sat around the campfire, the team discussed the day's findings. The possibility that they were on the trail of something truly unknown was both thrilling and unnerving. Dr. Ivanov, usually a bastion of skepticism, found himself entertaining the notion that they might be on the verge of a discovery that could challenge the established understanding of the region's wildlife.

The night brought with it a palpable tension, the darkness outside their tents seeming deeper, filled with the unknown. The distant howls and cries of the forest's nocturnal inhabitants now carried a different weight, a reminder of the fine line between myth and reality.

As dawn broke, casting a soft light through the dense canopy, the team awoke to find their campsite in disarray. Supplies were scattered, and peculiar markings were etched in the dirt, different from any animal tracks they had seen. The air was filled with a heavy sense of being watched, an unnerving sensation that they were not alone in this remote wilderness.

Determined to find answers, the team pressed on, following the trail that now seemed to be leading them not just through the physical landscape of Siberia, but through the layers of legend and myth that had long shrouded this land in mystery. The deeper they ventured into the forest, the more the line between the known and the unknown blurred, setting the stage for revelations that would challenge their understanding of the natural world.

Into the Heart of the Unknown

The Siberian wilderness, a labyrinth of ancient trees and hidden valleys, had always been a tapestry of mystery and folklore. Dr. Alexei Ivanov and his team, now several days into their expedition, were about to delve deeper into this enigmatic world than they had ever anticipated.

The trail they had been following, marked by the mysterious footprints and the occasional strand of coarse hair, led them to a rugged valley, cradled by towering cliffs. The beauty of the place was stark, almost haunting, with the silence of the forest punctuated only by the occasional cry of a distant bird.

As they navigated this new terrain, Dr. Ivanov noticed a shift in the wildlife behavior. The typically abundant sounds of the taiga had dimmed, as if the creatures themselves were wary of this part of the forest. Even the air seemed different here, heavier, as though it carried the weight of untold stories.

It was here, in a secluded glen surrounded by ancient cedars, that they made a startling discovery. Partially hidden under a layer of fallen leaves and moss, they found what appeared to be another larger makeshift shelter. It was constructed with a surprising level of skill, using branches and foliage woven together in a way that was neither entirely animal nor human.

The discovery was puzzling, blurring the lines between the known behaviors of animals and the legends of the Khomani. Dr. Ivanov, a scientist at heart, struggled to fit this finding into any conventional understanding of the region's fauna.

As the team set up camp near the shelter, a sense of unease settled over them. The twilight hours brought a chilling silence, a quiet so profound it felt like a prelude to something momentous.

That night, as they gathered around the campfire, their conversation turned to the legends of the Yeti. The local guide, a man of few words, shared tales passed down through generations, of a creature that was part of the land, a spirit of the taiga. These stories, once mere folklore to the team, now took on a new significance.

In the early hours of the morning, while the camp was steeped in sleep, Dr. Ivanov awoke to a faint rustling outside his tent. Peering out, he glimpsed a large, shadowy figure moving through the trees at the edge of the clearing. It moved with a deliberate, almost graceful gait, disappearing into the darkness before he could discern any details.

THE YETI, RUSSIAN YETI, SASQUATCH & BIGFOOT... 141

The following morning, Dr. Ivanov's account added a new layer of intrigue to their expedition. The team was abuzz with theories and speculation, but the scientist in Dr. Ivanov urged caution. Without clear evidence, he was reluctant to draw conclusions.

Determined to find more substantial proof, they spent the day exploring the area around the shelter. It was then that they found a series of markings on a tree trunk, at a height that suggested something much larger than any known animal in the region.

As they prepared to leave the valley, a sense of anticipation hung in the air. They were on the cusp of something extraordinary, a discovery that could redefine the boundaries of known science. The mysteries of the Siberian taiga, long shrouded in legend and folklore, were slowly revealing themselves, challenging the team to question what they thought they knew about the natural world.

The Unresolved Enigma

As the Siberian expedition led by Dr. Alexei Ivanov continued to traverse the dense, enigmatic landscape of the Kemerovo region, the boundary between the empirical world of science and the realm of the unknown grew ever more blurred. The discoveries made thus far – the inexplicable footprints, the mysterious shelters, and the fleeting glimpse of a shadowy figure – had injected an element of the extraordinary into their scientific endeavor.

On what would be the final day of their expedition, the team ventured deeper into a part of the forest where the thick canopy cast the ground into perpetual twilight. It was here, in this twilight realm, that they encountered the most compelling evidence yet. Nestled in a small clearing, partially obscured by ferns and underbrush, they found an object that defied easy explanation. It was a crude, yet distinctly crafted, tool, resembling a sort of primitive hammer or club, made from materials found in the forest.

Dr. Ivanov, upon examining the tool, found himself grappling with a multitude of questions. The craftsmanship suggested a level of intelligence and dexterity that was uncharacteristic of the region's known wildlife. Could this be a missing piece in the puzzle of the Khomani, a tangible link to the legend that had long captivated the imagination of the locals?

The team, their curiosity piqued, conducted a thorough search of the area, hoping to uncover further evidence. However, as the hours passed, it became apparent that this solitary artifact was all that the forest was willing to yield.

As they prepared to make their way back to civilization, Dr. Ivanov reflected on the expedition and its findings. The footprints, the shelter, the fleeting glimpse of the mysterious figure, and now the primitive tool – each discovery had added a layer to the mystery, yet none provided a definitive answer. The scientific part of him remained cautious, wary of drawing conclusions without irrefutable evidence. Yet, as a human, he couldn't help but feel that they had brushed against something truly unknown, a secret that the Siberian taiga was not yet ready to relinquish.

The journey back was quiet, each member of the team lost in their thoughts, processing the experience in their own way. The wilderness around them, once a vibrant tapestry of life and sound, now seemed to watch them in silence, its secrets guarded and unspoken.

Upon their return, Dr. Ivanov compiled the expedition's findings in a comprehensive report. The samples collected – the hairs, the photographs of the footprints, and the primitive tool – were subjected to rigorous analysis. Yet, despite the best efforts of modern science, the results were inconclusive and the Russian government chose to play down the reports, with the implication that Dr. Ivanov was an attention-seeking eccentric. The hairs could not be matched to any known species, the footprints remained a mystery, and the tool, while fascinating, did not provide the concrete evidence needed to draw a definitive conclusion.

In the end, the Siberian expedition left Dr. Ivanov and his team with more questions than answers and ruined Dr. Ivanov's career. The Khomani, the Yeti of Siberian legend, remained an enigma, a shadow lurking in the vast wilderness of the taiga. Dr. Ivanov, a scientist to the core, disappeared into obscurity after being forced to admit that the mystery of the Khomani was still unsolved, a puzzle piece in the vast and intricate tapestry of our planet's unexplored wonders.

Chapter 11
Debunking Yeti Myths: A Scientific Approach

The myth of the Yeti, a creature said to roam the Himalayan region, has been a subject of fascination for centuries. However, in the realm of science, the existence of the Yeti is viewed with a healthy dose of skepticism. This chapter examines the scientific approach to debunking the myths surrounding the Yeti, highlighting the methodologies and findings that have shaped our understanding of this legendary creature.

The Search for Scientific Evidence

One of the fundamental aspects of debunking Yeti myths is the quest for tangible, scientific evidence. Scientists have long sought physical proof of the Yeti's existence, such as DNA samples, clear photographic evidence, or biological specimens. Yet, despite numerous claimed sightings and anecdotal reports, no verifiable evidence has been presented that conclusively proves the existence of the Yeti.

Analysis of Alleged Yeti Evidence

Over the years, various materials purported to be from the Yeti have been subject to scientific analysis. For example, hair samples claimed to be from the Yeti were analyzed using DNA sequencing techniques. These studies often reveal that the samples belong to known animals, such as bears or other Himalayan wildlife. Similarly, alleged Yeti footprints, often cited as evidence, have been analyzed and often attributed to other causes, such as the melting and refreezing of snow that can distort animal tracks.

The Role of Misidentification

Misidentification plays a significant role in perpetuating the Yeti myth. In many cases, what is believed to be a Yeti sighting can be attributed to the misidentification of known animals, such as bears, which are native to the Himalayas and can walk bipedally, leading to confusion. Additionally, the challenging terrain and weather conditions of the Himalayas can lead to visual distortions and misinterpretations of natural phenomena.

The Influence of Local Folklore and Culture

Local folklore and cultural beliefs significantly influence the perpetuation of the Yeti myth. In many Himalayan communities, the Yeti is an integral part of local lore, often depicted as a guardian or spiritual entity. While these cultural narratives are rich and significant, they do not constitute scientific evidence of the Yeti's existence. Understanding the cultural context is crucial in distinguishing between myth and reality.

The Perspective of Skepticism and Rational Inquiry

A skeptical and rational approach is essential in debunking Yeti myths. This involves critically evaluating evidence, considering alternative explanations, and adhering to the principles of scientific inquiry. Such an approach helps in separating fact from fiction and ensures that conclusions are based on empirical evidence rather than speculation or anecdotal reports.

The scientific approach to debunking Yeti myths emphasizes the importance of evidence-based inquiry. While the Yeti continues to be a subject of popular interest and cultural significance, the lack of concrete scientific evidence challenges its existence as a real creature. The Yeti myth serves as a compelling case study in the application of scientific skepticism and rational analysis in exploring and understanding unexplained phenomena.

Scientific Skepticism: A Rational Approach

The investigation into the Yeti, a cornerstone of cryptozoology, offers a fascinating case study in scientific skepticism. Cryptozoology, the study of creatures like the Yeti whose existence is not substantiated, often finds itself at odds with mainstream scientific methodology. This dissonance raises significant questions about the nature of evidence, the role of speculation, and the boundaries between myth, folklore, and scientific inquiry.

Cryptozoology: Between Science and Speculation

Cryptozoology often treads a fine line between scientific inquiry and speculative fiction. A key issue in this field is the reliance on anecdotal evidence and eyewitness accounts, which are inherently subjective and difficult to verify. This approach contrasts sharply with the empirical methods central to conventional science, which rely on objective, repeatable observations and rigorous testing of hypotheses.

The field of cryptozoology has been criticized for often overlooking the fundamental principles of scientific research, such as quality data collection, documentation, and open criticism. It tends to be a mixture of low-quality evidence, hype, rampant speculation, and unfounded assumptions. For instance, cryptozoological writings sometimes present extinct species, such as post-Cretaceous plesiosaurs or nocturnal Neanderthals, as surviving in modern times without substantive evidence. These ideas, more aligned with speculative zoology or science fiction, lack empirical support and are not generally recognized by the scientific community.

A telling example is the cultural phenomenon surrounding various cryptids. Historical analyses of sea monster accounts reveal a shift in descriptions over time, aligning more with popular cultural depictions rather than biological reality. Prior to the mid-19th century, sea monsters were mostly described as serpent-like. However, following the public introduction and popularization of plesiosaurs in the scientific literature, descriptions of these monsters began to align more with the long-necked plesiosaurs. This suggests that public perception and cultural influence significantly shape cryptozoological reports, indicating a psychological or sociocultural basis rather than a zoological one.

The Role of Skepticism in Cryptozoological Research

Skepticism plays a crucial role in the scientific process, serving as a check against unfounded claims and speculations. In cryptozoology, skepticism often clashes with the beliefs of enthusiasts who are convinced of the existence of creatures like the Yeti without concrete evidence. This conflict highlights the importance of critical thinking and evidence-based analysis in scientific research.

Not all cryptozoologists are averse to skepticism. In fact, there are individuals within the cryptozoological community who maintain a commitment to data collection and respect for the scientific process. This demonstrates that even within fields often labeled as pseudoscientific, there can be a spectrum of approaches, ranging from the highly speculative to the more empirically grounded.

The study of the Yeti and other cryptids through the lens of scientific skepticism offers valuable insights into the workings of science and the importance of evidence-based reasoning. While the allure of mysterious creatures like the Yeti captivates the public imagination, the rigorous standards of science necessitate skepticism and critical analysis. The intersection of cryptozoology with mainstream science thus becomes a compelling dialogue about the nature of evidence, the role of belief in scientific inquiry, and the ever-evolving understanding of the natural world.

In essence, the rational approach to studying the Yeti and similar cryptids is not merely a dismissal of these legends but an invitation to scrutinize and understand the complex interplay between myth, culture, and science. The journey of cryptozoology, from fringe speculation to a subject of scientific scrutiny, reflects a broader narrative about the human quest for knowledge and the intricate pathways through which we seek to unravel the mysteries of our world.

The Skeptics' Viewpoint: A Critical Analysis

In the realm of Yeti research, skepticism plays a crucial role, functioning as a necessary counterbalance to cryptozoological claims. The examination of Yeti-related findings through a skeptical lens provides a deeper understanding of the scientific process and the nature of evidence. One notable instance in this discourse is the critical analysis of Bryan Sykes' DNA findings, which initially suggested a potential link between Yeti evidence and an ancient bear species.

Debating the DNA Evidence

Sykes' research, which analyzed hair samples attributed to Yeti and other anomalous primates, concluded that many of these samples belonged to bears and other non-mystery animals. However, this study faced significant criticism. Edwards and Barnett, in a response published by the Royal Society, contended that the match to ancient bear DNA might be misleading, suggesting that modern bear populations could contain similar genetic markers. This critique highlighted the possibility of DNA degradation and misinterpretation in Sykes' analysis.

In a subsequent study, Gutiérrez and Pine conducted a detailed comparison of bear DNA data and concluded that there was no evidence of a taxonomically unrecognized bear in the Himalayas. They suggested that the samples were more likely from the known Himalayan brown bear, Ursus arctos. This conclusion aligns with the broader skeptical perspective that Yeti legends may stem from bear misidentifications.

Beyond the Yeti: Understanding Misidentification

The skeptical viewpoint emphasizes the importance of considering misidentification in Yeti sightings. Despite some Yeti legends being rooted in bear encounters, these majestic and dangerous animals do not closely resemble humanoid figures, particularly upon close examination. This perspective shifts the focus from the search for a mysterious creature to understanding the psychological and cultural factors influencing people's perceptions and reports.

The Role of Skepticism in Cryptozoology

Skeptical analysis in cryptozoology is not an outright dismissal of the possibility of unknown species but a rigorous questioning of the evidence. It is a call for applying scientific methodologies to testable questions within the field. This approach is vital in navigating the complex interplay between folklore, cultural narratives, and scientific inquiry. While it challenges the more speculative aspects of cryptozoology, it also underscores the need for robust evidence and critical thinking in exploring the unknown.

The skeptics' viewpoint offers a critical analysis of Yeti research, emphasizing the need for scientific rigor and cautious interpretation of evidence. It highlights the importance of considering alternative explanations, such as misidentification and cultural influences, in understanding cryptozoological claims. This perspective is integral to maintaining a balanced and evidence-based approach to the study of the Yeti and similar cryptids, contributing to a more nuanced understanding of the natural world and our perceptions of it.

Critical Scientific Analysis: Debating the Yeti

The Yeti, a creature of legend and folklore, has long been the subject of scientific debate. This chapter delves into the critical analysis of scientific efforts to uncover the truth behind the Yeti phenomenon, exploring both the cultural and biological aspects of this enigmatic being.

The Cultural Context of the Yeti

The Yeti, often portrayed as an ape-like glacier spirit, has deep roots in the mythology and folklore of the Himalayan region. Indigenous groups like the Lepcha people view the Yeti as a powerful entity with influence over their lives, such as the success of hunting trips. These cultural narratives imbue the Yeti with qualities that blend the real and the supernatural, making it a complex figure in Himalayan society. This cultural significance has shaped the way the Yeti is perceived, blurring the lines between myth and reality.

Scientific Investigations into Yeti Claims

In recent years, several scientific investigations have aimed to demystify the Yeti. One significant study involved the genetic analysis of supposed Yeti samples (including hair, bones, and scat), which revealed that most of these samples belonged to known bear species, particularly the Himalayan and Tibetan brown bears. This finding dispels many myths surrounding the Yeti while providing valuable insights into the genetics and evolutionary history of these bear species.

For instance, the research led by Charlotte Lindqvist, a professor specializing in species genetics, examined mitochondrial DNA from nine alleged Yeti samples. The study concluded that seven of these samples came from Himalayan or Tibetan brown bears, one from a black bear, and one from a dog. This research not only challenged the Yeti myth but also shed light on the genetic diversity of bear species in the Himalayas, with implications for conservation efforts.

The Yeti in the Realm of Spurious Science

The field of cryptobiology, which includes the study of the Yeti, often oscillates between genuine scientific discovery and speculative inquiry. Bryan Sykes, a geneticist from the University of Oxford, contributed to this debate by comparing DNA from two hair samples found in the Himalayas to those of known animals. Initially, Sykes reported a match with ancient polar bear DNA, fueling speculation about a possible Yeti-bear hybrid. However, further examination and peer reviews suggested that the samples more likely belonged to the Himalayan brown bear, a conclusion that aligns with the majority of scientific findings on the Yeti.

The critical scientific analysis of the Yeti bridges cultural narratives and biological facts, offering a multi-faceted understanding of this legendary creature. While the myth of the Yeti continues to captivate the human imagination, scientific inquiries have largely demystified its existence, pointing instead to the misidentification of known wildlife. This intersection of myth, culture, and science not only informs our understanding of the Yeti but also highlights the dynamic relationship between human belief systems and the natural world. Through this lens, the Yeti emerges not just as a subject of folklore, but as a catalyst for scientific curiosity and exploration.

Controversial Theories and Myths: Nazi Expeditions and Beyond

The intersection of Yeti lore with the dark chapters of history, particularly involving the Nazis, forms a controversial and often misunderstood narrative. The exploration of this topic reveals a complex blend of myth, political ambition, and scientific curiosity.

Nazi Expeditions in Search of the Yeti

During the late 1930s, the Nazis, under the leadership of Heinrich Himmler and driven by their occult interests and pseudo-scientific theories, embarked on expeditions to various parts of the world, including the Himalayas. The most notable of these was the 1938-1939 German expedition to Tibet, led by Ernst Schäfer, a German zoologist and SS officer. This expedition, ostensibly for scientific and cultural research, has been surrounded by rumors and speculations about its true purpose, including the quest for the Yeti.

Schäfer and his team collected a vast array of scientific data, including thousands of specimens of plant and animal life, extensive ethnological and topographical information, and a wealth of photographic and film material. However, despite the abundant documentation, there is no concrete evidence to support the theory that the expedition's primary goal was to find the Yeti. Instead, the records suggest a focus on the collection of natural history specimens and cultural artifacts.

The Myth of the Nazi-Yeti Connection

The idea that the Nazis were specifically searching for the Yeti as part of their expeditions is largely speculative and not supported by historical records. The narrative seems to have evolved from the confluence of the Nazis' well-documented interest in the occult and the enduring allure of the Yeti myth. The expeditions were more likely driven by a combination of political, military, and scientific objectives, rather than a singular focus on cryptid hunting.

The Yeti in the Context of Nazi Ideology

The association of the Yeti with Nazi expeditions also touches upon the broader theme of how myth and pseudoscience were exploited for political purposes. The Nazis were known for their fascination with Aryan mythology and their attempts to link their racial ideologies to various myths and legends. While the Yeti itself was not directly implicated in these narratives, the expeditions to regions like Tibet were part of a larger effort to establish cultural and scientific dominance aligned with Nazi beliefs.

The intertwining of the Yeti legend with Nazi history is a topic shrouded in myth and speculation. While the Nazi expeditions to Tibet and the Himalayas were real and well-documented, the evidence does not support the theory that finding the Yeti was a primary goal. Instead, these expeditions reflect a complex interplay of scientific inquiry, political ambition, and the exploitation of myth for ideological purposes. The Yeti, in this context, remains a creature of folklore, its legend inadvertently magnified by its association with one of the most controversial chapters of the 20th century.

Iconic Yeti Sightings and Evidence: A Critical Review

The quest for the Yeti, a creature deeply enshrined in myth and folklore, has yielded a mix of intriguing evidence and controversial claims. Two of the most iconic pieces of evidence in Yeti research are the Shipton Footprints and the Khumjung Scalp.

The Shipton Footprints

In 1951, during a reconnaissance expedition in the Himalayas, British mountaineer Eric Shipton photographed a series of unusual footprints in the Menlung Basin, Nepal, at an altitude of 16,000-17,000 feet. These footprints, measuring 12-13 inches long and twice the width of an adult man's foot, with distinct toes and a depth suggesting a weight greater than a human's, captivated the world. Although natural phenomena and wildlife activity could explain these prints, their unique features have made them a cornerstone of Yeti lore.

The Khumjung Scalp

Another notable artifact is the Khumjung Scalp, housed in a monastery in the Nepalese village of Khumjung. Acquired by Edmund Hillary during his 1960 Yeti hunting expedition, this scalp was initially thought to be a groundbreaking piece of Yeti evidence. However, scientific analysis later identified it as the hide of a serow goat, a revelation that tempered the excitement but didn't entirely extinguish the hope of Yeti enthusiasts.

The search for the Yeti has been marked by moments of wonder, skepticism, and scientific inquiry. While no definitive proof of the Yeti's existence has been found, the enduring fascination with these iconic pieces of evidence reflects the human desire to explore the unknown and the allure of the mysteries that might be hidden in the remote corners of our planet.

The Yeti and Tourism: Impact on Local Communities

The allure of the Yeti has not only fueled a global fascination but has also significantly impacted tourism in regions associated with these legendary creatures. This impact is multifaceted, encompassing economic, social, cultural, and environmental dimensions.

Economic Benefits of Yeti-Related Tourism

Yeti-related tourism has brought considerable economic benefits to local communities. This impact can be understood through the lens of the multiplier effect, where tourist spending stimulates local economies. Tourists visiting areas known for Yeti legends often engage in various activities like trekking, cultural tours, and purchasing local goods. This spending helps to generate revenue for local businesses, which can then reinvest in their services, enhancing the attractiveness of the destination and creating a positive cycle of economic growth. This growth leads to job creation in sectors like accommodation, food and beverages, and tourism activities, providing employment opportunities for local residents.

Furthermore, tourism revenue can facilitate infrastructure development. This includes improvements in transportation, accommodation facilities, and access to tourist attractions. Such development not only serves tourists but also enhances the quality of life for the local population.

Social and Cultural Benefits

Tourism can play a significant role in preserving and showcasing cultural heritage. In regions known for Yeti folklore, there is an opportunity to promote cultural tourism, which involves visitors experiencing and learning about local culture, traditions, and legends like that of the Yeti. This form of tourism can motivate communities to maintain and display their unique cultural assets, contributing to cultural preservation and pride.

Improved quality of life often follows the economic benefits of tourism. Increased income from tourism can lead to enhanced living standards, including better wealth, material goods, comfort, and services. Additionally, tourism can foster social cohesion by creating opportunities for people from different socioeconomic backgrounds to collaborate and work towards a common goal.

Environmental Benefits and Challenges

Yeti-related tourism can also contribute to environmental benefits, particularly in the context of ecotourism and responsible tourism. These forms of tourism emphasize the conservation of natural resources and wildlife, which are often the main attractions in Yeti legend areas. By generating income from preserving natural landscapes and biodiversity, communities are incentivized to maintain these resources.

However, tourism can also pose challenges, such as environmental degradation, cultural erosion, and social issues. Addressing these challenges requires careful planning and the implementation of sustainable tourism practices that minimize negative impacts while maximizing benefits.

Case Studies of Yeti-Related Tourism Impact

Specific examples of communities that have benefited from Yeti-related tourism can be seen in various parts of the Himalayas, where local agencies collaborate to promote sustainable travel that respects local communities, wildlife, and the environment. Companies like Yeti Holidays are committed to supporting local projects that improve the quality of life, particularly in remote regions associated with Yeti legends. They engage in responsible tourism practices, ensuring that their activities do not adversely affect the local environment and community.

The legend of the Yeti has not only captivated imaginations worldwide but has also brought tangible benefits to local communities where these legends are prevalent. By harnessing the potential of tourism, these regions have seen improvements in their economies, infrastructure, social cohesion, and cultural preservation. However, the key to sustaining these benefits lies in responsible and sustainable tourism practices that respect and protect the unique cultural and environmental heritage of these areas.

Cross-Cultural Comparisons: Global Yeti Legends

The Yeti, a creature shrouded in mystery and intrigue, is not just a singular myth confined to the Himalayas. Its legend spans across various cultures, each with its unique interpretation and lore. This chapter delves into the cross-cultural comparisons of Yeti legends, exploring how different societies perceive this enigmatic creature.

The Yeti in the Himalayas

In the Himalayan region, the Yeti, also known as the 'Abominable Snowman,' is often depicted as a large, ape-like creature dwelling in the snowy peaks. Local lore describes it as a solitary and elusive being, occasionally leaving large footprints in the snow. Sherpas and other indigenous peoples of the region regard the Yeti with a mix of reverence and fear, often associating it with spiritual and natural elements.

The Sasquatch of North America

Across the globe in North America, the Sasquatch or Bigfoot shares striking similarities with the Yeti. Indigenous North American tribes have long spoken of a large, hairy, bipedal creature inhabiting the forests, particularly in the Pacific Northwest. Sasquatch is often described as a nocturnal creature, known for its immense strength and elusiveness, much like the Yeti.

The Yowie of Australia

In Australian folklore, the Yowie emerges as a parallel to the Yeti. Described in Aboriginal myths as a hairy, ape-like creature residing in the Australian wilderness, the Yowie is said to be both shy and ferocious. Reports of Yowie sightings mirror those of the Yeti and Sasquatch, with descriptions focusing on its large footprints and towering presence.

The Almasty of Central Asia

Central Asia has its variant of the Yeti known as the Almasty. Folklore from regions like Mongolia and Russia describe the Almasty as a wild humanoid creature, covered in hair and living in the mountainous terrains. Though reports of the Almasty are less common, they contribute to the broader narrative of ape-like cryptids across cultures.

Interpretations and Explanations

The cross-cultural existence of Yeti-like creatures raises intriguing questions about human psychology and the understanding of our natural environment. Some anthropologists suggest that these legends could be a form of collective memory, preserving encounters with now-extinct hominids. Others interpret these myths as personifications of wilderness and nature's unknown aspects.

Moreover, these legends also reflect each culture's relationship with its environment. Whether as a symbol of unexplored wilderness or as an embodiment of natural mysteries, the Yeti-like creatures serve as a reminder of the vast, uncharted territories that still exist in our world.

The global phenomenon of Yeti legends, spanning from the Himalayas to North America and beyond, illustrates the universality of human myth-making and our fascination with the unknown. These cross-cultural narratives, while varying in details, all speak to a shared human experience - an enduring intrigue and awe for the mysteries that lurk in the remote corners of our planet. The Yeti, in all its forms, continues to captivate our imagination, serving as a powerful symbol of the wild and unexplored realms of nature.

Global Yeti Phenomenon: Cultural and Economic Impact

The Yeti, a legendary creature often depicted as a large, ape-like being, has not only fascinated people around the world but also significantly influenced various cultures and economies. This impact transcends the mere pursuit of a mythical creature; it encompasses a broader spectrum of cultural, economic, and sociological effects.

Cultural Impact of the Yeti Legend

1. **Mythology and Folklore**: The Yeti, known in various cultures under different names (Bigfoot in North America, Yowie in Australia, and Almas in Mongolia), is deeply rooted in the folklore of many societies. These legends often reflect the relationship between humans and their natural environment, illustrating an inherent curiosity about the unknown and a respect for the mysteries of nature.

2. **Literature and Media**: The Yeti has been a popular subject in literature and media, often portrayed in books, films, and television shows. This portrayal has significantly influenced public perception of the creature, oscillating between a fearsome beast and a misunderstood entity living in harmony with nature.

Economic Impact of the Yeti Phenomenon

1. **Tourism**: Regions known for Yeti sightings, such as the Himalayas, have experienced a boost in tourism. Adventurers and enthusiasts flock to these areas in hopes of encountering

the elusive creature, contributing to local economies through trekking tours, accommodations, and the purchase of related merchandise.

2. **Research and Expeditions**: Funding for expeditions and research into the existence of the Yeti has provided economic opportunities for scientists, local guides, and support staff. These activities not only contribute financially but also help in the conservation of remote areas and the study of biodiversity.

Sociological Effects

1. **Community Identity and Pride**: In regions where Yeti legends are prevalent, such as the Sherpa communities in Nepal, these legends form a part of their cultural identity and heritage. The Yeti is often a source of community pride, reinforcing a unique cultural identity.

2. **Cultural Exchange**: The global interest in the Yeti has encouraged cultural exchange. Tourists and researchers engaging with local communities in search of the Yeti often learn about local customs, traditions, and perspectives, fostering a better understanding and appreciation of diverse cultures.

Conservation and Environmental Awareness

The search for the Yeti has inadvertently highlighted the need for conservation and environmental protection. Remote areas, often the settings for Yeti legends, are ecosystems rich in biodiversity. The increased attention from Yeti enthusiasts has raised awareness about the importance of preserving these pristine environments.

The global Yeti phenomenon is a remarkable example of how a legend can transcend its mythical origins to impact real-world cultural, economic, and environmental landscapes. Whether viewed as a symbol of the unknown, a cultural icon, or a catalyst for exploration and conservation, the Yeti continues to captivate the global imagination, leaving an indelible mark on societies worldwide.

Chapter 12
The Ecological Impact of Cryptids

The concept of cryptids, like the Yeti, and their ecological impact present an intriguing area of study that intertwines mythology, conservation, and environmental science. While cryptids themselves are not recognized as real entities in scientific taxonomy, the pursuit of these mythical creatures can have unexpected benefits and implications for ecological research and conservation efforts.

1. **Inspiration for Biodiversity Exploration**: The search for cryptids often leads to remote and unexplored regions, which can result in the discovery of new species or a better understanding of known species. For instance, the quest for the spiral-horned ox, a cryptid, involved classic cryptozoological methodologies such as analyzing folklore and historical accounts. This not only furthers our understanding of biodiversity but also highlights the vastness of undiscovered life forms on our planet.

2. **Conservation Awareness**: Interestingly, the fascination

with cryptids like the Yeti can raise public awareness about the importance of conservation. As people become intrigued by these legendary creatures, they inadvertently learn about the ecosystems these creatures are believed to inhabit. This can lead to increased support for conservation initiatives in these areas.

3. **Shared Histories with Conservation Movements**: The history of cryptozoology has intersections with conservation movements. Notable figures in conservation, such as Peter Scott, founder of the World Wildlife Fund, showed interest in cryptids. Such interest can sometimes lead to conservation efforts, as was the case with Scott's interest in the Loch Ness Monster, where he aimed to protect the hypothetical creature under conservation laws.

4. **Enhancing Ecological Understanding**: While the existence of cryptids like the Yeti is highly debatable, the pursuit of these creatures can enhance our ecological understanding. The methodologies used in cryptozoology, such as gathering local folklore, examining physical evidence, and conducting field surveys, can provide valuable insights into local ecosystems and biodiversity.

5. **Promotion of Ecotourism**: In regions famed for their cryptid legends, such as the Himalayas for the Yeti, ecotourism can flourish. This not only helps in conserving these regions but also promotes sustainable tourism practices. Visitors drawn by the lore of cryptids can contribute to the local economy and become advocates for the preservation of these natural habitats.

6. **Cryptids as Ecological Indicators**: The study of cryptids, although speculative, can sometimes act as an indicator of ecological health. For example, tales of lake monsters might bring attention to the conditions of the lake ecosystems and the need to preserve them. Similarly, forest-dwelling cryptids like the Yeti could draw attention to the health of forest ecosystems.

7. **Educational Value**: The lore of cryptids can be used as an educational tool to engage the public, especially the younger audience, in ecology and environmental science. The captivating stories of these creatures can be a gateway to teaching about real-world biodiversity, conservation, and the importance of protecting our natural world.

While the existence of cryptids like the Yeti remains within the realm of mythology, their conceptual and cultural presence has real-world implications for ecology and conservation. The fascination with these mythical creatures can inadvertently lead to positive ecological outcomes, such as the discovery of new species, increased conservation awareness, and a greater appreciation for our planet's biodiversity.

Conservation and Cryptid Research: Environmental Aspects

The intersection of conservation and cryptid research, though seemingly disparate fields, offers an intriguing blend of mythological pursuit and ecological awareness. While cryptids like the Yeti are largely considered mythical, the search for these creatures can inadvertently contribute to environmental conservation efforts.

Cryptid Research and Biodiversity Exploration

1. **Exploration of Remote Habitats**: Cryptid research often leads explorers and scientists into remote and uncharted natural habitats. This exploration, while primarily aimed at finding mythical creatures, can result in the discovery of new species and ecosystems, enriching our understanding of biodiversity.

2. **Increased Awareness of Endangered Species**: The fascination with cryptids can bring attention to real, endangered species inhabiting the same regions. For instance, while tracking alleged Yeti habitats, researchers may encounter threatened species, thus highlighting the need for their protection.

3. **Contribution to Ecological Studies**: Cryptid research methodologies, like analyzing folklore, historical accounts, and conducting field surveys, can provide valuable ecological data. These studies can offer insights into the flora and fauna of the region, contributing to broader ecological research.

Conservation Efforts Influenced by Cryptid Research

1. **Habitat Preservation**: The search for cryptids can lead to the preservation of vast tracts of land. By declaring these areas as potential habitats for mythical creatures, they inadvertently become protected zones, thereby conserving the local biodiversity.

2. **Ecotourism Development**: In regions famed for cryptid legends, ecotourism can flourish. This not only benefits local economies but also promotes sustainable tourism practices, which are crucial for conservation. The interest in cryptids can drive visitors to these areas, who then contribute to the local conservation efforts either directly or indirectly.

3. **Promotion of Environmental Education**: Cryptid legends can be an effective tool for environmental education. They provide a unique angle to engage the public, especially younger audiences, in discussions about wildlife conservation, habitat protection, and the importance of biodiversity.

Challenges and Ethical Considerations in Cryptid Conservation

1. **Balancing Myth and Reality**: One of the primary challenges in merging cryptid research with conservation is the balance between mythological pursuit and scientific reality. Ensuring that conservation efforts are grounded in scientific evidence is crucial for their credibility and effectiveness.

2. **Avoiding Misuse of Conservation Resources**: There's a need for careful consideration to ensure that resources allocated for conservation are used effectively and not misdirected towards chasing mythical entities without any scientific basis.

3. **Ethical Use of Cryptid Narratives**: While cryptid stories can be leveraged for conservation purposes, it is essential to

ethically use these narratives. They should not overshadow the real and pressing issues faced by actual endangered species and their habitats.

While the primary focus of cryptid research might be the pursuit of mythical creatures like the Yeti, it inadvertently contributes to environmental conservation. This unexpected intersection offers opportunities for biodiversity exploration, habitat preservation, and ecological awareness. However, it's vital to approach this blend of mythology and ecology with scientific rigor and ethical considerations to ensure effective and sustainable conservation efforts.

The Yeti Yonder

The exploration of the Yeti mystery, often referred to as the "Yeti Yonder," encompasses not only the pursuit of this elusive creature but also delves into the broader cultural and psychological fascinations that surround it. This chapter explores various aspects of this phenomenon, from historical encounters and scientific investigations to its impact on popular culture and the human psyche.

The Yeti in Historical and Cultural Context

The Himalayan Yeti, deeply rooted in the mythology of the Himalayan region, has been a subject of awe and reverence. Different ethnic communities, including Sherpas and Tibetans, have their unique interpretations of the Yeti, often portraying it as a supernatural being with immense strength and protective qualities. The creature is believed to have the ability to camouflage itself in its environment, making it exceptionally elusive. These cultural narratives have significantly shaped the Yeti's identity as a symbol in local folklore and beyond.

Scientific Investigations and Controversies

Numerous scientific expeditions have attempted to demystify the Yeti. Theories have ranged from it being a rare species of bear with bipedal tendencies to a surviving hominid or a unique primate. The lack of concrete evidence, however, leaves the scientific community largely skeptical. One notable expedition was led by Sir Edmund Hillary in 1960, which discovered a peculiar skull initially thought to belong to the Yeti. Later DNA analysis identified it as belonging to a rare Tibetan antelope, debunking one of the most controversial Yeti-related claims.

The Yeti in Modern Media and Public Perception

The Yeti has transcended its origins as a cryptid to become a fixture in modern media and popular culture. Its portrayal in movies, animations, and literature has evolved from a fearsome creature to a figure of intrigue and mystery. This shift in portrayal reflects a broader change in public perception, transforming the Yeti from a creature of horror to a symbol of the unknown and the unexplored.

Human Fascination with the Unknown

The allure of the Yeti can be attributed to a deep-seated human fascination with the extraordinary and unexplainable. This fascination is reflected in various forms of art, narrative, and even technology. The concept of the Yeti captures our collective imagination, tapping into our desire to explore and understand the mysteries of our world. It serves as a reminder of the uncharted territories that still exist and the inherent human urge to uncover what lies beyond the known.

The Future of Yeti Research and Conservation

As technology advances, the nature of Yeti research and the mysteries surrounding it are likely to evolve. Despite skepticism and the prevalence of hoaxes, the possibility of future 'real' encounters with creatures like the Yeti cannot be entirely dismissed. This ongoing intrigue underscores the importance of preserving these legends as part of our cultural heritage and the natural world. The future of Yeti research thus lies not just in proving or disproving its existence, but in maintaining a balance between discovery and the preservation of mystery.

The Yeti Yonder represents more than just the pursuit of a cryptic creature; it embodies the human quest for understanding the unknown. It challenges our perceptions of reality and spurs a continuous dialogue between myth and science, between fear and fascination. As we explore the Yeti's mysteries, we are reminded of the enduring power of legends and the endless scope of human curiosity.

Chapter 13
Modern Mythology

The intertwining of mythology and the human psyche offers a profound insight into our understanding of reality and self. This chapter explores the intricate relationship between myth, reality, and the human psyche, examining how these elements interact to shape our perception of the world and ourselves.

The Psychology of Myth

The essence of mythology lies in its ability to represent human experience artfully. A myth cannot be entirely true or false; it captures aspects of human experience in a narrative format. These stories resonate with us because they reflect our emotions and ambitions, such as the tales of Icarus and Phaethon, which echo the youthful tendencies to aim too high and the resultant consequences. This storytelling aspect is crucial to human memory and understanding. Memory is not a literal replay of events but a reconstructive storytelling process, where events are restructured into a coherent narrative. This narrative construction is a natural way for the mind to make sense of the world, often adding or omitting details to fit an overall pattern.

The Role of Myth in Understanding the Human Psyche

Ancient Greek myths, particularly those involving the psyche, delve deep into the human soul, highlighting emotions and psychological states. These myths offer insights into human behavior, feelings, and psychological disorders, emphasizing values like love, compassion, and forgiveness. By exploring these myths, we gain a deeper understanding of the human psyche and the role of emotions in our experiences. Stories like that of Eros and Psyche or Odysseus and Circe not only entertain but also educate us about the complexity of human emotions and responses.

The Impact of Secularization and Rationalization

With the advent of secularization, the supernatural elements of myths have often been downplayed, interpreted as allegory or instructive fables. In a science-driven society, it's easy to dismiss myths as literally untrue. However, this perspective misses the point of what myths are and their role in human experience. Myths are about the soul's endless journey and the adventure into the self, helping us understand our psychology better. They bind communities through shared experiences and ceremonies, reminding us that we are part of something larger than ourselves.

Mythology in Modern Times

In contemporary times, the role once played by soothsayers and mystics in interpreting myths has been taken up by psychoanalysts. Psychoanalysis, much like ancient mythology, bridges the gap between the conscious and the unconscious. By analyzing dreams and unconscious desires, psychoanalysts help us make sense of our world and our experiences, akin to the spiritual awakening found in mythological hero journeys. These journeys of introspection, much like the hero touching the metaphorical face of God, transform the individual, highlighting the enduring power of mythology in our lives.

The exploration of the relationship between mythology and psychology reveals how deeply intertwined these aspects are in shaping our understanding of ourselves and the world. Mythology, through its narrative and allegorical nature, provides a framework for understanding the human psyche, offering insights into our emotions, behaviors, and the very fabric of our being. As we continue to delve into the mysteries of the human mind, the lessons and insights from ancient myths remain as relevant and illuminating as ever, guiding us in our quest for self-understanding and growth.

Global Perspectives on the Unknown: A Yeti Case Study

The global fascination with the Yeti, often termed the "Abominable Snowman," represents a unique intersection of myth, science, and cultural curiosity. This chapter delves into various aspects of Yeti research and perspectives from around the world, analyzing the interplay between legend and scientific inquiry.

Scientific Investigations and Genetic Studies

In recent years, the study of the Yeti has transitioned from folklore to a subject of serious scientific inquiry. Notably, genetic studies have played a pivotal role in demystifying some aspects of the Yeti legend. A significant study involved examining the mitochondrial DNA of supposed Yeti samples. In total, nine purported Yeti samples were analyzed, including items such as teeth, hair, and scat, some dating back to the 1930s. The results of these analyses were revealing: seven samples came from Himalayan or Tibetan brown bears, one from a black bear, and one from a dog.

These findings highlight the importance of the Himalayan brown bear, a unique creature of ancient lineage, in the Yeti narrative. This species, critically needing conservation attention, has inadvertently gained prominence due to its association with Yeti mythology.

Iconic Yeti Evidence: Footprints and Scalp

The legend of the Yeti has been fueled by various pieces of 'evidence' over the years. Among the most notable are the Shipton footprints, discovered in 1951 by British mountaineer Eric Shipton in the Menlung Basin, Nepal. These footprints, measuring 12-13 inches long and unusually wide, with peculiar toes, sparked significant interest and debate. The photographs of these prints were considered some of the first substantial Yeti evidence.

Another intriguing piece of Yeti lore is the Khumjung scalp, which came to Western attention through explorer Edmund Hillary. Housed in Nepal's Khumjung monastery, this relic was initially thought to belong to the Yeti. However, scientific scrutiny over the years has cast doubt on its authenticity as a Yeti artifact.

Global Perception and Cultural Impact

The Yeti has transcended its origins in Himalayan folklore to become a global phenomenon. This "glacier spirit" has captured the imagination worldwide, becoming a minor deity of sorts in the human consciousness. The Yeti's fame is a testament to the enduring power of myth and the human fascination with the unknown. This global attention has not only spurred scientific investigations but also highlighted the unique ecology and culture of the Himalayas.

The Yeti case study presents a fascinating blend of myth and reality, where scientific inquiry meets ancient legend. While the scientific community has provided rational explanations for many Yeti-related findings, the creature's mythic stature continues to captivate imaginations globally. The Yeti narrative, therefore, remains an intriguing mix of cultural folklore, scientific exploration, and environmental awareness, reflecting humanity's enduring quest to understand the mysterious and the unknown.

Reflecting on the Journey: Science, Myth, and Spirit

The exploration of the Yeti has journeyed through the realms of mythology, folklore, and scientific inquiry, revealing a fascinating intersection of cultural beliefs and scientific understanding. This chapter reflects on the journey of Yeti research, highlighting its impact on both science and cultural perception.

The Intersection of Culture and Science

The Yeti, a central figure in Himalayan lore, has been a subject of intrigue and mystery for centuries. Western interpretations of the Yeti often viewed it through a lens of cryptozoology, similar to the Loch

Ness Monster. However, this perspective may overlook the cultural and spiritual significance the Yeti holds in Himalayan societies. In these cultures, the Yeti is often seen as more than a mere physical being; it is a spiritual entity, a glacier spirit, and a deity in the complex spiritual world of the Himalayas. This cultural context suggests a rich tapestry of belief where mythical beings like the Yeti are intertwined with the everyday life and spiritual practices of local communities.

Scientific Revelations and Misunderstandings

The scientific investigation into the existence of the Yeti has yielded significant insights, particularly in the field of genetics. Studies have focused on analyzing DNA from various samples attributed to the Yeti, including hair, bones, and feces. These studies often revealed that most of these samples belonged to local animals, particularly the Himalayan and Tibetan brown bears. This research not only demystified some aspects of the Yeti legend but also brought to light the genetic uniqueness and evolutionary history of these bear species. The Himalayan brown bear, for instance, was found to be one of the earliest diverging lineages of modern brown bears.

The Broader Impact on Conservation and Understanding

The pursuit of the Yeti has inadvertently drawn attention to the ecological and conservation needs of the Himalayan region. By uncovering the genetic history of local bear species, scientists have highlighted the importance of these animals in the region's biodiversity and the need for their conservation. This research has demonstrated the interconnectivity of myth, biodiversity, and environmental awareness, showing how legendary creatures can foster an understanding of real, yet often overlooked, species.

The journey of Yeti research embodies a unique blend of mythological belief, cultural understanding, and scientific inquiry. It reveals how myths can lead to tangible scientific discoveries and highlights the importance of respecting and understanding cultural contexts in scientific exploration. The case of the Yeti serves as a reminder of the complex relationships between humans, our myths, and the natural world we inhabit.

Echoes of Discovery

The exploration of the Yeti, a creature deeply rooted in the folklore and mythology of various cultures, especially in the Himalayas, has led to a fascinating journey of discovery, bridging the gap between myth and science.

Cultural Significance and Interpretation

The Yeti, often portrayed as an ape-like creature, holds a place of profound importance in the folklore and mythology of the Himalayan region. In local lore, it is more than a physical entity; it embodies spiritual and cultural aspects that are deeply interwoven with the lives and beliefs of the people. The Yeti is often seen as a symbol of the unknown and the unexplored, representing the mysteries that nature still holds. The myth of the Yeti reflects the human fascination with the unknown and the allure of exploring uncharted territories.

Scientific Pursuit and Discoveries

The scientific study of the Yeti has been a journey of debunking myths while simultaneously uncovering important ecological and evolutionary information. Genetic analyses of purported Yeti samples, such as hair, bones, and fecal matter, have often led to the identification of local wildlife, particularly the Himalayan and Tibetan brown bears. This research has contributed to our understanding of these species' genetic diversity and evolutionary history, indicating their critical need for conservation. The exploration of the Yeti myth has inadvertently fostered a deeper understanding of the biodiversity in the Himalayas.

Broader Implications

The pursuit of the Yeti has had broader implications, particularly in highlighting the relationship between myth, biodiversity, and environmental awareness. Myths like that of the Yeti can serve as catalysts for scientific exploration, leading to discoveries that extend beyond the initial scope of the myth. This journey underscores the importance of considering cultural narratives and folklore in scientific research, as they can provide valuable insights into the natural world and contribute to conservation efforts.

The exploration of the Yeti is a testament to the enduring intrigue and mystery that mythical creatures hold for humanity. It exemplifies how myths and folklore can lead to significant scientific discoveries, enriching our understanding of the natural world. The Yeti's story is a reminder of the intricate interplay between culture, science, and the environment, urging us to continue exploring the unknown with a sense of wonder and respect for both the legends of old and the scientific truths they may unveil.

The Evolution of Yeti Lore: From Ancient Myths to Modern Day

The Yeti, also known as the Abominable Snowman, has evolved from ancient myths to a modern-day cultural icon, captivating the imagination of people worldwide. This chapter delves into the transformation of Yeti lore, examining its origins, cultural significance, and the impact of scientific inquiry on this legendary creature.

Origins and Cultural Significance

The Yeti, a figure deeply entrenched in the Himalayan lore, has been part of the region's mythology for centuries. Initially, the Yeti was more than just a creature; it was a symbol deeply embedded in the spiritual and cultural fabric of the Himalayan people. Local folklore often depicted the Yeti as an ape-like glacier spirit, influencing various aspects of life, including hunting. These tales, rich in cultural and spiritual significance, presented the Yeti as a being that transcended the physical realm, intermingling the real and the mythical.

Western Encounter and Misinterpretation

The Western world's encounter with the Yeti lore began in the early 20th century when explorers returned from the Himalayas with intriguing tales of the mysterious beast. This encounter led to a shift in the perception of the Yeti, from a revered cultural symbol to a subject of cryptozoological interest. Western interpretations often failed to grasp the complex cultural context of the Yeti myth, reducing it to a mere cryptid akin to the Loch Ness Monster. This misinterpretation highlighted the cultural disconnect and the lack of understanding of the Himalayan spiritual and mythological landscape.

Impact of Scientific Inquiry

Recent scientific studies have significantly impacted the Yeti lore. DNA analysis of artifacts attributed to the Yeti, such as hair and bone samples, revealed that these items belonged to local bear species, including the Himalayan brown bear and the Tibetan brown bear. This revelation dispelled many myths about the Yeti's physical existence while shedding light on the genetic and evolutionary aspects of these bear species. The scientific community's involvement in Yeti research demonstrates the potential of modern science to tackle mysteries and unsolved questions, offering rational explanations for what was once considered purely mythical.

Modern Cultural Phenomenon

Despite the scientific debunking of its physical existence, the Yeti continues to thrive as a cultural phenomenon. It remains a popular figure in urban legends, myth, and cryptozoology. The Yeti's enduring appeal lies in its mystery and the human fascination with the unknown. It is a testament to the power of folklore and its ability to transcend time, evolving from ancient myths to a symbol of mystery and exploration in modern culture.

The evolution of Yeti lore from ancient myths to its current status in modern culture highlights the dynamic interplay between folklore, culture, and science. The Yeti's journey is a reflection of humanity's enduring curiosity and the desire to understand the unknown, bridging the gap between myth and reality.

The Yeti in Digital Storytelling: New Age Narratives

In the realm of digital storytelling, the Yeti has emerged as a prominent character, offering a blend of mystery, intrigue, and folklore in modern narratives. This chapter explores how the Yeti is portrayed in digital media, examining its evolution from a mythical creature of ancient tales to a vibrant figure in contemporary digital narratives.

Emergence in Digital Media

The Yeti's transition into digital storytelling marks a significant shift in how this mythical creature is perceived and portrayed. In digital media, the Yeti is often depicted with a blend of mystique and charisma, appealing to a global audience that craves adventure and exploration. Digital platforms, including movies, video games, and interactive websites, have embraced the Yeti, often incorporating it into storylines that blend folklore with modern themes. These portrayals have significantly influenced how the Yeti is viewed by contemporary audiences, transforming it from a creature of lore to a character in mainstream entertainment.

The Yeti in Video Games and Interactive Media

In video games and interactive media, the Yeti often appears as a character that players must confront or understand. These games create immersive experiences, allowing players to engage with the Yeti in virtual environments that mimic the creature's supposed natural habitat. This interactive aspect of digital storytelling enables a deeper connection with the myth, as players actively participate in unfolding narratives that revolve around the Yeti. Through these mediums, the Yeti is not just a passive character in a story but an integral part of interactive adventures and challenges.

The Yeti in Online Narratives and Social Media

The proliferation of social media and online platforms has given rise to new forms of storytelling where the Yeti features prominently. Online narratives, whether in the form of webcomics, digital art, or social media posts, often use the Yeti as a symbol of the unknown or as a metaphor for various human experiences. These digital stories sometimes reimagine the Yeti in contemporary settings, merging ancient lore with modern-day scenarios, thereby creating a unique blend of the traditional and the modern. The Yeti's presence in these narratives showcases its versatility as a character that can transcend time and cultural boundaries.

Educational and Cultural Significance

Digital storytelling has also utilized the Yeti for educational purposes. Interactive educational programs and documentaries available online often use the Yeti as a focal point to explore themes such as biodiversity, conservation, and cultural folklore. By featuring the Yeti, these educational narratives aim to spark curiosity and encourage learning, especially among younger audiences. Additionally, they provide cultural insights into the regions associated with Yeti folklore, highlighting the importance of preserving cultural heritage and folklore in a rapidly modernizing world.

The Yeti's foray into digital storytelling represents a fascinating aspect of its evolution. Through modern digital media, the Yeti continues to captivate and intrigue audiences worldwide, transcending its origins as a mythical creature of the Himalayas to become a versatile character in new age narratives. This evolution not only entertains but also educates, bridging the gap between ancient folklore and contemporary culture, and ensuring that the legend of the Yeti remains alive in the digital era.

The Yeti and the Search for Truth: Between Fact and Fiction

The Yeti, a legendary creature of the Himalayas, has been a subject of intrigue and scientific inquiry, representing a unique intersection of myth and reality. This chapter delves into the evolution of Yeti lore, the scientific pursuit for truth, and the balance between belief and skepticism in understanding this enigmatic being.

Evolution of Yeti Lore

The legend of the Yeti dates back thousands of years, deeply rooted in the cultures surrounding the Himalayan mountain range. Initially, the Yeti was more than a cryptid; it was a part of the pre-Buddhist beliefs of the Himalayan peoples, often worshipped as a god of the hunt. The Western world's fascination with the Yeti began in the early 20th century when explorers returned from the Himalayas with tales and supposed evidence of this mysterious creature. The Yeti, thus, transitioned from a regional myth to a subject of global curiosity and speculation.

Scientific Inquiry and Genetic Discoveries

The quest to validate the existence of the Yeti has led to numerous scientific investigations, particularly in the field of genetics. A notable study involved DNA analysis of artifacts claimed to be from the Yeti, including teeth, bones, hair, and skin. These analyses revealed that most artifacts were actually from local bear species, including the Asian black bear, the Tibetan brown bear, and the Himalayan brown bear. This revelation not only demystified some aspects of Yeti lore but also contributed significantly to the understanding of bear evolution in the Himalayas.

Balancing Belief and Skepticism

While science provides a rational lens to view the Yeti legend, it does not entirely diminish the cultural and mythical significance of the creature. The Yeti remains an essential part of Himalayan folklore, embodying a bridge between the known and the unknown. This duality of the Yeti, as both a subject of scientific scrutiny and a mythical entity, highlights the complex relationship between fact and fiction in our understanding of the world. The Yeti's story serves as a reminder of the enduring human fascination with the mysterious and the unexplained.

The journey of understanding the Yeti is a reflection of humanity's quest for knowledge, balancing skepticism with respect for cultural narratives and myths. The Yeti, whether a myth or a misunderstood animal, continues to captivate the human imagination, symbolizing our unending pursuit of the unknown.

The Yeti in World Religions: Sacred and Profane

The Yeti, often recognized in the West as the Abominable Snowman, holds a significant position in the religious and mythological beliefs of the Himalayan region. This chapter explores the Yeti's role in these beliefs, particularly in Tibetan mythology.

Tibetan Mythology and the Yeti

In Tibetan folklore, the Yeti is more than a legendary creature; it represents a deep connection with the spiritual and natural world. The Yeti is seen as a guardian spirit of the Himalayan peaks, embodying the sacredness of these mountains. It symbolizes the untamed and wild nature of the high-altitude wilderness, representing mysteries and unexplored realms within the natural world. In this context, the Yeti transcends the boundaries of mere folklore, becoming a symbol of protection, the wilderness, and a link between the physical and spiritual realms.

The Yeti in Religious Context

The Yeti is integrated into the polytheistic and inclusive religious traditions of the Himalayan region, where older folk beliefs and deities are absorbed over time, creating a complex spiritual world. This perspective includes a range of deities and spirits, from major gods to minor entities responsible for specific aspects of life, such as guarding a river crossing or one's home. The Yeti, in this context, is often viewed through the lens of these diverse and rich spiritual traditions.

The Yeti in world religions, particularly in Tibetan mythology, is not just a mythical creature but a significant symbol interwoven with the spiritual beliefs and cultural practices of the Himalayan people. Its depiction in these religions reflects a deeper understanding of the sacred and the profane, illustrating how myths and folklore can hold profound religious and spiritual significance.

The Yeti and the Future: Predictions and Possibilities"

As we look towards the future, the Yeti's place in science, culture, and environmental discourse presents a rich field for speculation and exploration. This chapter delves into the possibilities and predictions regarding the Yeti's role and representation in the coming years, considering the impacts of scientific advancements, cultural shifts, and ecological concerns.

Scientific Advancements and Cryptozoology

The future of Yeti research is likely to be shaped significantly by advancements in scientific methodologies, particularly in genetics and ecology. As DNA sequencing becomes more sophisticated and accessible, it opens the door to new possibilities in verifying or debunking cryptid claims. In the case of the Yeti, further genetic analysis of alleged physical evidence could either cement its status as a mythical creature or perhaps reveal unexpected truths about undiscovered species in remote environments.

Cultural Shifts in Mythology and Storytelling

Culturally, the Yeti is poised to evolve within our collective narratives. As global connectivity and cultural exchange increase, so does the potential for the Yeti myth to assimilate new characteristics and interpretations. This could lead to a richer, more diverse set of stories and representations, potentially influencing everything from literature and film to virtual reality experiences. The Yeti's role as a symbol of the unknown and the wild may also gain new relevance in an increasingly digital and urbanized world, reminding us of the mysteries that still exist in nature.

Environmental and Conservation Perspectives

The Yeti's future is also inextricably linked with ecological and conservationist efforts, particularly in the Himalayan region. The myth of the Yeti draws attention to these remote and often fragile ecosystems, highlighting the need for their preservation. The Yeti legend could serve as a powerful tool for environmental advocacy, promoting awareness and protection of biodiversity in the Himalayas. As climate change and human activities continue to impact these regions, the Yeti's symbolic power could play a crucial role in rallying support for conservation efforts.

Looking forward, the Yeti remains a fascinating subject at the intersection of myth, science, and environmentalism. Its future will likely be shaped by a combination of scientific discovery, cultural evolution, and ecological challenges. Whether as a mythical symbol or a subject of scientific inquiry, the Yeti will continue to captivate and inspire, reminding us of the vast and mysterious natural world that surrounds us.

Chapter 14
Concluding Echoes: The Lasting Mystery of the Yeti

As we conclude this exploration of the Yeti, it's clear that this enigmatic creature transcends its mythical origins, permeating various facets of science, culture, and spirituality. From its roots in ancient folklore to its presence in modern narratives and scientific discourse, the Yeti continues to captivate the human imagination.

The Yeti's Enduring Mystery

The Yeti remains a symbol of the unexplored and the unknown, embodying the human quest for understanding the mysteries of our world. Despite scientific efforts to demystify its existence, the Yeti still holds a place of wonder and intrigue. This enduring mystery not only fuels ongoing exploration and research but also keeps alive the rich tapestry of folklore and myth in which the Yeti is deeply woven.

The Yeti's Role in Future Discourse

Looking forward, the Yeti's legacy is likely to evolve, adapting to changes in scientific understanding, cultural narratives, and environmental awareness. The Yeti's story is more than just a quest to prove or disprove its existence; it is about preserving the sense of mystery and awe that is vital to our human experience. The discussions surrounding the Yeti will continue to reflect our evolving relationship with nature, science, and the realms of the unknown.

In conclusion, the Yeti, whether a creature of flesh and blood or a construct of human imagination, remains an integral part of our cultural and scientific narrative. It challenges us to ponder the boundaries between reality and myth and encourages us to keep exploring the vast and mysterious world around us. The Yeti's tale, therefore, is not just about the pursuit of a mythical beast but about the enduring human spirit of curiosity and wonder.